The Business Survival Kit

Byron Cole is a serial award-winning entrepreneur, public speaker, investor, philanthropist and business mentor. He has been involved in over fifteen business startups as a director, investor or shareholder. Byron is an investor in people, property and businesses of all types. He co-authored *Self-Made* with his wife, Bianca Miller-Cole, and is a co-host on their podcast of the same name.

Bianca Miller-Cole is an award-winning entrepreneur, global keynote speaker and 'top 10 powerful leader' on LinkedIn, and she uses her experience to assist budding entrepreneurs through her platform, book and podcast, *Self-Made*. She started her personal branding company, The Be Group, in 2012, and works with clients including Deloitte, AMEX, Google, Facebook, EY, Accenture, Clifford Chance and many more to inspire workforce potential. In 2014 she founded a groundbreaking hosiery company, which went on to be the first to offer an inclusive range of colours on the high street. Bianca spends much of her time mentoring entrepreneurs to support them in creating thriving enterprises.

The Business Survival Kit

Your No-BS Guide to Success

BYRON COLE AND
BIANCA MILLER-COLE

BUSINESS

PENGUIN BUSINESS

UK | USA | Canada | Ireland | Australia
India | New Zealand | South Africa

Penguin Business is part of the Penguin Random House group of companies
whose addresses can be found at global.penguinrandomhouse.com.

First published 2021
001

Set in 12/14.75pt Dante MT Std
Typeset by Jouve (UK), Milton Keynes
Printed and bound in Great Britain by Clays Ltd, Elcograf S.p.A.

The authorized representative in the EEA is Penguin Random House Ireland,
Morrison Chambers, 32 Nassau Street, Dublin D02 YH68

A CIP catalogue record for this book is available from the British Library

ISBN: 978–0–241–44739–0

Follow us on LinkedIn: https://www.linkedin.com/company/penguin-connect/

www.greenpenguin.co.uk

MIX
Paper from
responsible sources
FSC® C018179

Penguin Random House is committed to a
sustainable future for our business, our readers
and our planet. This book is made from Forest
Stewardship Council® certified paper.

To Everyone Working Hard to Build a Better Life
and a Legacy for You and Your Family.
This Book Is Dedicated to You.

Contents

Acknowledgements

Byron

First of all, I would like to give thanks to God.

To my amazing wife, rock, co-author and business partner, Bianca. No long speech required. Thank you and I love you.

A special tribute goes to team Penguin, not only for making this journey so smooth but also for giving us the platform to get these important messages out to the world.

I would like to thank my mentees, past and present. You guys are my motivation and inspiration in so many different ways. Keep rising, keep shining and smash those goals – nothing can stop you.

I can't let this moment go without thanking my social media followers and #byronites who support me unconditionally.

I would like to thank each and every one of you that has supported me along my journey.

I hope you all enjoy this book. We created this for YOU.

To your Success,

Byron – I live to Inspire

Bianca

Thank you to everyone who bought our first book, which resulted in the development of our 'Self Made' mentoring community. The feedback from our readers and mentees inspired us to write this book. We recognize now that there is so much that goes unwritten and unsaid about the realities (and perils) of being in business. Starting a business is one thing; surviving and thriving while running a business is very much another. You all helped me to see that and realize it is a reality that needed to be articulated more widely. Witnessing your growth continues to motivate me to do and learn more.

Byron, you continue to wear many hats in my life – as my best friend, soulmate, husband, co-author, major supporter and business partner. Our partnership continues to blossom because we are on the same page, writing each chapter in the book of our lives together – our way! Thank you.

To my parents, I am who I am because of you, and for that I will always be grateful. I love you both.

To my clients, I've been talking about 'intrapreneurship' for years. I am so pleased you have embraced it. Thank you for trusting me.

To everyone who is currently reading this, don't let anyone say you can't. You can AND you will!

Joint Thanks

We have so many friends and family, we would love to name you all but that would be impossible, so instead we would like to thank you all from the bottom of our hearts for your continuous love and support – you know who you are.

To our interviewees, industry experts, Martina, Trevor and everyone who helped us put this book together, we would like to extend a special thank you to you all. And to our team, who embrace our every business move.

Preface: Forget 'Business as Usual'

There is no 'usual' in business. Each business has its own voice, narrative and capabilities, as do the people who are at its forefront. Whether you are reading this as a business owner, a budding entrepreneur, an employee dedicated to your career, or a student – you are the most important asset in any venture. And we have created this book for you, to help you understand the emotional rollercoaster of being in business and the 'business of you'.

Business isn't easy – it takes guts, it takes grit, it takes the odd tearful moment, but along with what might sometimes appear to be earth-shattering lows are the amazing highs that make it all worthwhile.

This is not a book that exists purely to tell you 'yes, you can do it'. You already know if you can or can't (and if you don't, you will by the end of the book). Rather, this book tells you *how* to do it. It provides you with the coping mechanisms, strategies and support you need to make it happen.

Oh, and it will probably prove to you that you are not alone. Every emotion, feeling and issue you encounter has probably been experienced by every person around you . . . the difference being, we aren't afraid to talk about it in this book. Business is hard, but we're here to hold your hand on the rollercoaster.

So, here we go . . . we're going to look at purpose, clarity, anxiety, procrastination, romantic conflict, sleep deprivation, imposter syndrome, and so much more. It will be emotional and sometimes difficult. It will also be a lot of fun. The secret is to know how to roll with the punches.

Join us on the journey. This is business as *un*usual.

Introduction

Running a company – particularly if it's your first time – involves a steep learning curve.

And that's OK. You've undoubtedly accepted that there will be an enormous amount to learn. You're going to have to get to grips with market research, preparing a business plan, raising money to get you through the first few months, hiring staff, and a whole host of other things. Yes, you'll be in uncharted territory, but you've got a pretty good idea of what's involved. You know what to expect.

But we're here to tell you that there will be surprises – not least because you'll be learning a huge amount about yourself and how you handle difficult and often stressful situations. It's this personal aspect of running a company that most business guides tend to ignore, sidestep or underplay.

On one level, that's entirely understandable. If you're starting out on the entrepreneurial road, you absolutely need to know how to construct a credible business plan, master sales, build a personal brand and set up the accounting systems that will keep the tax authorities happy. Equally, once the venture is up and running, it's vital that you understand how to manage cash flow, build infrastructure or even prepare the business to be sold. We covered all of that and more in our first book, *Self Made*.

But the technical side of running a business only represents part of the story. As an entrepreneur, you are typically putting heart, soul and, very possibly, your life savings into your chosen venture. And that's an emotional thing.

It's Emotional

From the day you launch, your company is the cause that you fight for. To make it a success, you'll work long hours, miss family events and have to live with the fact that the dividing line between a good and a bad outcome depends, to a very great extent, on your judgement.

Along the way, you'll face a whole range of obstacles – some of them relatively easy to negotiate, and others with the potential to run your dreams on to the rocks. You'll find that making the right call is not always easy. Indeed, it can be difficult even to see a situation clearly. Most likely, there will be times when it all seems too much. So much so that you feel like giving up, or spend months wrestling with insecurities and anxieties.

There is, however, almost always a way through.

That was a lesson we learned when putting together our first book – *Self Made: The Definitive Guide to Business Startup Success*. Written as a toolkit for entrepreneurs, it is an action-oriented guide for those who need as much information as possible about the mechanics of setting up a company. It was something of a labour of love, and an opportunity to give something back by sharing the knowledge and information we'd amassed over our years running successful companies.

But the journey from conception to bookshop shelves wasn't straightforward. We had a literary agent pitch the idea to a number of publishers – small and large – and initially failed to generate much interest. That could have been the end of the story, but it wasn't. Realizing that it was perfectly possible to self-publish, we decided to write *Self Made* anyway. In addition – and this was crucial – we also developed a business plan to ensure the book would sell and make money. Our plan A had morphed into plan B. We weren't going to give up.

Once the book was written, the situation changed again. With everything completed, we realized we now had something traditional publishing houses wanted to buy. So, having put in the work, we were back on track with our original plan. The book got a publisher and went on to be a bestseller – not only in the UK, where we're based, but in many other places around the world.

The whole process reminded us that success is not just about having a great product that fills a gap in the market. You also need the mindset and sense of purpose that will see you through when it seems the whole world is saying no.

In a very real way, the story of the *Self Made* journey contained the seeds of the book that you are about to read. Rather than being a startup guide, this is a survival kit – one that will tell you what it's really like to pursue a business dream. Looking beyond processes, best practices and quantifiable skills, this book focuses on the personality, drive and inner toughness required by the entrepreneur. It is about facing difficulties, making decisions – very often hard ones – and overcoming self-doubt and other deep-seated emotions that can hold you back.

It's also about relationships with people. No entrepreneur is an island. Even if your business consists of just you and a laptop, you'll be talking to customers and suppliers, probably on a daily basis. If you run a bigger company, you may have one or more partners and possibly also investors, in addition to a team of employees. In all cases, there are relationships to be managed, and inevitably there will be times when not everyone is in agreement or alignment. Managing people, and conflict, is an important part of an entrepreneur's life.

As is crisis management. Witness the Covid-19 pandemic. This was something that most of the world just didn't see coming. In the space of a few short months, a functional global economy was brought to its knees. Near the beginning of the crisis, 3.9 billion people (or half the world's population) were in lockdown, according to United Nations figures.

For many small businesses, the economic meltdown came out of the blue. There was no warning. And yet, even in the hardest-hit sectors, we saw resilience. Restaurants pivoted to takeaway and home delivery businesses. Training companies moved from physical sessions, with dozens of people gathered together in a room, to the safety of video conferencing via Zoom, Google or Microsoft Teams. Retailers stepped up their mail-order businesses. Where possible, owners, managers and the wider workforce stayed at home, but carried on working.

It would be wrong to say that every agile and innovative business managed to survive, but it's certainly true that those which were prepared to adapt and pivot had a much greater chance of navigating a course through the obstacles of the pandemic.

Mindset

It's tempting to think that a successful mindset is something intrinsic to the individual – to assume that while some people have a will to overcome hurdles, others give up when faced by adversity. That it's just who they are, after all.

In reality, our personalities and personal attributes are not set in stone. We can all take steps to improve the way we respond to situations and interact with those around us. To put it another way, we can all develop and grow. We can all make ourselves better entrepreneurs.

This book will provide you with the information you need. Every challenge that you'll face as you grow your business has been experienced by other entrepreneurs. You won't be the first to lose a major customer. The economic downturn generated by the pandemic was unprecedented but there have been numerous recessions in the post-war years, including the great financial crash of 2007–2008. In the face of adversity, businesses survived and even thrived.

At a less dramatic level, a great many entrepreneurs have struggled with walking into a crowded room to network with complete strangers. Equally, there is no shortage of entrepreneurs who have wrestled with the stresses caused by success, perhaps from finding themselves running businesses that are bigger and more complicated than they ever intended.

There is no need to reinvent the wheel every time you face a challenge. There are plenty of existing strategies, tactics and life hacks that will help you realize your dream. We're here to show you what they are.

How to Use This Book

At the core of this book is our dual experience as entrepreneurs – each pursuing our own business ambitions while supporting the other. To reflect those twin perspectives, each of us has taken the lead in writing separate chapters. It's an approach that has allowed our individual voices to come through, while avoiding the trap of writing chapters by committee. Perhaps more importantly, it has allowed us to emphasize aspects of business life that have particularly engaged us as individuals, while also highlighting the experiences that are common to just about every entrepreneur.

This is not intended to be a coffee-table book – although you are more than welcome to leave it on a table or in some other prominent position. Nor is it intended to be read once and then filed away on a bookshelf, never to be seen again.

Quite the opposite. This is a practical guide to help you at every stage of your entrepreneurial journey. It is packed with exercises, entrepreneur insights, tools, techniques and other thought-provoking content. Read it through once and you'll get a lot out of it, but we suggest that you keep it at hand. And what we really want you to do is refer to it constantly, thumb through it, bend back the pages, make notes in the margins. In five years' time, if it's lying on your desk looking a bit ragged and the worse for wear, with some of the pages coming away from the binding, we won't hold it against you. In fact, we'll take it as a compliment. The book will have done its job in helping you to better understand yourself, your stakeholders and how to steer your business through good, bad and perhaps chaotic times.

Read and Reread

Ideally, you should start out by reading the book in the order it was written; this approach will provide the best overview of some of the challenges that lie ahead. But don't feel you have to. Business is not linear. Everyone hits bumps in the road, but not everyone experiences the same obstacles at identical points on the entrepreneurial journey. So if you are faced with a particular problem, find the relevant chapter and jump right in. After that, you can go back to reading in sequence.

Take Notes

It can be a bit too easy to read a book on Monday and forget most of the main points by Friday. The best way to engage is to become an active reader. Take notes. It doesn't matter whether you jot them down in the margins, keep a separate journal or write them on a Post-it which you then attach to the page. The main thing is that you are interacting. This not only helps you to remember the content but also allows you to add your own thoughts and experiences, making the book's insights more relevant.

Remember to have some paper to hand too. We've included a range of exercises throughout the book, designed to help you crystallize your thoughts as a way of preparing for action. But it's important to remember that every business is different. If you come across an exercise that doesn't square with your experiences, feel free to adapt it – again, make it relevant.

It's also well worth revisiting the exercises as your business grows and changes. To give you an example – goal setting is a constant in business. Today, you might be aiming for a £50,000 turnover, and to achieve that you'll need to set a series of goals to help you reach that ambition. But what happens when you hit £50,000? Then you'll need new goals, strategies and tactics. You can use our goal-setting template again and again.

Social Media

Don't keep your insights to yourself. As you move forward with the help of this book, share your progress, your experiences and your ups and downs on social media. Other people will want to know. And, guess what, you'll build a community that can only help you to achieve your ambitions in the longer term.

Stay in Touch

We want to know about your progress too, so don't forget to stay in touch with us. We would really like to hear stories of your self-made journey and how this survival guide has helped you.

You can connect with us on:

Instagram: Bianca: @biancamillerofficial; Byron: @mrbselfmade; and the community on @selfmadebookuk.

Podcast platforms/YouTube: The Self Made Book Channel is available for free across all platforms.

Email: Office@selfmadebook.uk – If you have any feedback or wish to share your journey with us, we would love to hear from you, so please do send us an email. Our favourite part of writing books, mentoring and delivering workshops is being able to hear people's success stories, so we would love to hear from you about how the book has helped along your journey.

Website: www.selfmadebook.uk – This is where you will find lots of free business resources, event listings, details about our mentoring programme, and access to our online courses.

Chapter One

Define Your Purpose

*'If you can't figure out your purpose, figure out your passion.
For your passion will lead you right into your purpose.'*

– T. D. Jakes

You're an aspiring entrepreneur. You're launching a business. For the moment at least, your course is set.

But I've got some news for you. While this may be your first business venture, it almost certainly won't be your last. At some time in the future, you may well start a second business, and then a third. In the meantime, as you move forward with your current venture, things will evolve. Inevitably, you will adapt your plan and perhaps even pivot to a completely new business model, as circumstances and your own assessment of the opportunities change. In two years' time, you may not have the same business that you started out with. It could be (almost) unrecognizable.

Byron and I see this with our mentees all the time. They come to us with a carefully developed business concept. As we work with them, their plan develops and ultimately morphs into something that is often completely different.

This process of change and adaptation is necessary and positive, but it can lead to a period of uncertainty and perhaps self-doubt. As you ring the changes, you might well ask yourself: 'Is this what I signed up for – is this the right business for me?' This could be a recurring question. It's certainly something you should ask yourself at the beginning of your entrepreneurial journey, when you are thinking about how to turn your idea into a fully fledged and profitable venture.

Later, when your business has been up and running for a while, you may well pause for breath and say: 'Hold on, this isn't the business

I started with. Is this something I want to go on doing?' Further down the line, as your business grows and you have an opportunity to expand and take on more staff, you will find yourself faced with unfamiliar challenges – for instance, running a twenty-strong team when at the beginning it was just you and a partner. You'll need to ask yourself if this is what you wanted or expected when you started out – or has it grown into something that is stressing you out rather than making you happy?

You Always Have Options

Here's the good news: as an entrepreneur you always have options. If you don't think a business plan is quite right, you can change it. If the business is moving in a direction you're uncomfortable with, you can alter the course. *You* are in the driving seat. You have choices.

Let's look at an example. The entrepreneurial boom that has taken place over the past decade has focused attention on a certain kind of business – one that could be characterized as a 'build and sell' venture. Essentially, we're talking about founders who start out with the express aim of selling the business at some point in the future, so their priority is to grow revenues very quickly, which in turn pushes up the value of the company ahead of their exit. To finance the growth plan, the owner will often sell shares in the business to venture capitalists (VCs) or angel investors, who are also keen to cash in via an exit.

It's easy to see why this kind of company attracts the attention of the media. Everyone loves to hear about big numbers, whether that's 25 per cent annual growth, a £500,000 investment or a £15 million sale. Figures like this make for big, sexy stories that speak of the dynamism of not only the founders but also the investors. In contrast, 'lifestyle' businesses that make a profit and do pretty well, but not spectacularly, attract very little attention. Indeed, they can even be disparaged.

And that's wrong. A successful business can be anything you

want it to be. If your goal is to grow, take investment, and cash in for a life-changing sum of money, that's absolutely great. But it's equally fine if you simply want to make a good living, work the business for most of your life and pass it on to your family. The choice is yours. You have an opportunity to be the entrepreneur that you always dreamed of being.

Paul Jarvis sums it up well. Based in Canada, he is co-founder of Fathom, a relatively small but very successful privacy analytics company. In addition, he is author of *Company of One*, a book that makes the case for staying small. He stresses the importance of making choices that are right for the individual. 'Success is personal,' he says. 'I didn't want to go after someone else's version of success. I didn't want to be like Elon Musk. He has a couch in his office where he sleeps at night. I also have a couch, but that's so I can take a nap from time to time.' Crucially, Jarvis's own lifestyle goals have dictated the kind of business he runs.

We can all do this. The key to getting it right is to find your purpose.

Is This Business Right for Me?

Let's take a closer look at the core question – namely 'Is this business right for me?' It seems simple, but there's actually a lot to consider.

You could express the answer purely in terms of viability. Will this business not only survive but flourish? For instance, is there a fit between the product and the market? Is the market big enough to generate a sufficient profit? In other words, you need to address some important commercial questions. And if the business plan simply doesn't add up, clearly it won't be the right venture.

But beyond viability, there is something more personal to think about. Maybe the venture will be a rip-roaring success, but that doesn't necessarily mean it's something you should be pursuing. There are plenty of people who have successful careers – as lawyers, board-level executives, doctors – but who would dearly love to do something different. Maybe they were pushed into those jobs by parents, or made choices based on their best subjects at school. Or perhaps they took the first job they could after leaving education, stuck with it and did well. But, at heart, they would rather be developing a career that offers more meaning.

It's the same in business. You can build a company that is financially a success – and who would argue with wanting that – and yet feel that you would rather be on a different course. And, actually, you might be more successful if you truly follow your own vision. For instance, there could be two identical entrepreneurial businesses, both selling the same product to broadly the same group of target customers. One flourishes, the other struggles. What differentiates them? In all probability, it is the passion, commitment and talent of the owners, rather than anything about the product itself. The fit between owner and business is important.

Why Purpose Matters

In addition to considering the commercial potential of a venture, it is vital to reflect on how the business sits with you as an individual. How does it map on to the person you are? Is this something that you can see yourself doing not just for two or three years, but for the long haul? That's important, because businesses can take years to fulfil their full potential.

So, ask yourself:

- Why do I want to start a business?
- What is my purpose as an individual?
- What is the purpose of the business, and how does it align with my purpose?

At this point, you might conclude that the answer is simple. Your purpose is to make money. The business exists to make money. It's a perfect pairing. But actually, the purpose isn't money. Certainly, one of your goals could be to achieve financial independence – or to put it another way, make a lot of money. But – and this is a big but – the purpose of a business has to be bigger than that. A business has to serve its customers, meet a need in the market, create a buzz, establish a brand. And from that perspective, money in itself isn't a purpose. Money is the outcome of successfully articulating and delivering on a clearly defined purpose.

Validating the Idea

Let's begin with the business itself – and its purpose.

It all starts with an idea. Maybe it's just a flash of inspiration on a drive home from a nine-to-five job, or maybe it's something that you've been thinking about for months or years. Initially, it's only a concept. You have an idea for a product or a service and you've identified a base of customers. What you don't know is whether or not it will work. So, there's an obvious first question to ask yourself: 'Is this the right idea?'

Answering this can be a bit like marking your own homework. You assemble a business plan, do some market research, work out how much it will cost to get the project up and running, and it all seems good. The problem is, you could be missing quite a lot of key information, especially if this is a first-time venture (and a step into the unknown) or a market you're not familiar with. Perhaps you talk to a few friends, and because they don't want to offend you or rain on your parade, they say, 'Great idea – go for it.'

Of course, there may be other friends who are equally fond of you and consequently want to save you from yourself. So while they're not exactly critical – as in, telling you it's a rubbish idea – they encourage you to consider how well you're doing in your current job and how much of a risk starting a business would be.

In other words, you have yea-sayers and naysayers. Neither group will necessarily provide useful advice – especially if they know very little about running a business themselves, or the market you are proposing to enter – but they will happily give the advice anyway. The moral of the story is, be careful who you accept advice from.

Expert Help

It's important to seek advice from people who can help you validate your idea by looking at it objectively and bringing their expertise and experience to the table. Typically, the most useful input comes from people who have enjoyed success in a similar field.

Let's look at an example. It can't have escaped anyone's attention that the world of media is evolving rapidly. One hugely significant manifestation of that change is the growth in the podcast market. Now, podcasts can be monetized in a lot of different ways, including advertising sales, sponsorship, and direct patronage from listeners and viewers. If you have a big enough audience, you can make a lot of money. So, these days, starting a podcast is a perfectly viable business proposition – all you need is a laptop, a decent microphone, a camera (if you're thinking video too) and some editing software, and you're on your way to becoming a media mogul.

If you can find and successfully monetize your audience, that is. Which isn't necessarily easy when there are thousands of other podcasts available around the world, all competing for attention. You can make great content, but there are a host of other things to consider, not least marketing and attracting advertisers and sponsors. If you are a media outsider – or even an insider who doesn't know a huge amount about the commercial side of podcasting – then you're probably going to need help.

The first thing to do is to look around your personal network. Is there anyone you know who understands the podcast space? Byron and I are very lucky in this regard, as one of our close friends has just signed a lucrative podcast deal with Spotify. When we need advice on our podcast activities, he is our first port of call. As a friend, he's happy to help.

But sometimes you won't necessarily need help that is industry-specific. For instance, you might need advice on raising finance to support your venture. What's required here is knowledge of the corporate finance market – bank loans, crowdfunding, selling shares, etc. – and a solid awareness of what potential investors or lenders are looking for. This might come from a corporate finance expert, or someone who has personally raised money. To give another personal example, one of our friends – Ash Ali – played a pivotal role in floating the food delivery company Just Eat on the stock exchange, through an initial public offering (IPO). If we were considering an IPO, he would be happy to provide advice.

Reaching out to suitably experienced people within your circle is a great way to at least make a start on validating your idea.

Building a Network

Now, admittedly, Byron and I are fortunate in that we know a lot of people who can provide expert advice and help fill in any gaps in our knowledge. But it wasn't always like that. It's worth remembering that, as you progress in your entrepreneurial career, your network will grow. In fact, you should begin the process of networking and building up contacts as soon as you possibly can. (We'll be dealing with this in Chapter Six.)

But let's assume for a moment that you don't have anyone that you can immediately turn to. That needn't be a problem. There is a huge amount of business expertise that can be accessed easily through networking groups and business associations.

Crucially, there is also LinkedIn. With more than 700 million users worldwide, it is a vital resource. The social media platform exists to help its registered users connect with others and develop their careers. You can use it to make contact with people in your prospective industry, or with those who are experts in, say, marketing or raising finance.

A bit of research is required – which can be done through

LinkedIn's search tool – but it is fairly easy to identify people who could be helpful to you. You can then send a connection request or message them directly. Alternatively, LinkedIn is home to a growing number of industry-specific forums. They are a great way to tap into virtual networks. You simply join, contribute and begin to make contacts.

Finding a Mentor

You shouldn't be afraid to ask for help. One common trait of successful people is that they are often happy to provide nuggets of advice, without expecting anything in return. There are limits, however. We are talking about busy people, who have their own businesses to run. So, always be polite and don't expect too much.

Nor should you be afraid to pay for the help you need. Indeed, unless you know a business mastermind really well, this may be the only way to get in-depth support. There are plenty of options, ranging from agencies providing specific services – market research, for example – to generalist consultants. But if you're looking for support in the longer term, it is worth seeking out a mentor.

If you work – or have worked – within a large organization, you may already have been part of a mentoring programme. Often, companies provide mentoring at points of change – for instance, when staff members are promoted to a higher level and are thus facing new and unfamiliar challenges. Typically, a mentor will be someone who understands those challenges and can provide support and practical help.

The same principle applies to the mentoring of entrepreneurs. The global entrepreneurship boom has created a vast and growing community of successful business leaders. All of them have encountered and overcome challenges along the way, in addition to picking up a great deal of technical expertise. Working with a mentor can help you identify opportunities, deal with difficulties and avoid many of the mistakes that you might otherwise make.

It would be wrong to characterize the mentor/mentee relationship purely in terms of teacher and pupil. It is that, to a degree, but a mentor will often be getting as much – or almost as much – from the relationship as their mentee does.

In a recent interview, author and inspirational speaker Simon Sinek described his relationship with his mentor, Ron Bruder, an older and more experienced entrepreneur. As Sinek recalled, the two men got talking and found they got along. At a later date, Sinek rang to seek advice. 'He took my call . . . And then he took my call again. And then we met for lunch.'

The relationship developed to the point where the younger man felt emboldened enough to say: 'I love that you're my mentor.' Bruder responded that he loved being Sinek's mentor. The respect was a two-way street. Mentors are teaching, but they are simultaneously learning. Which perhaps explains why so many busy and in-demand business people are not only willing but keen to mentor up-and-coming talent.

It's important to mention that individuals taking part in mentoring programmes also stand to benefit from peer-to-peer interaction. For instance, the programme that Byron and I run brings together entrepreneurs who are at different stages on their business journeys. Some are just starting out; others are running companies with a turnover of £5–6 million. They meet during our group mentoring sessions and also work with us privately. They are also connected via our WhatsApp community group and have a video-conferencing 'power hour' at 5.30 a.m., when they can collectively work on their businesses without interruption. As such, they benefit from a huge amount of peer-to-peer support while also building an all-important personal network. Crucially, everyone is seeking to help everyone else, while also getting mentoring from experienced entrepreneurs.

Optimism and Inspiration

The more you talk about your business – particularly with friends or acquaintances who won't necessarily be looking at your plans through analytical and professional eyes – the likelier you are to encounter negativity. There are a lot of naysayers out there, and you need to be able to deal with critical comments.

But what does that mean in practice? Well, neither Byron nor I would ever suggest that you should be blindly optimistic. We won't tell you to go ahead and do something without first having a good look at your proposition. Nor should you ignore anyone who points out the holes or flaws in your plan, because when someone waves a red flag, it's worth considering that the naysayer in question might just be right.

Because the truth is, it's always good to listen to those who raise valid points of concern. You may decide to agree to disagree, and press on regardless. On the other hand, you may realize the naysayer has picked up on something you've missed. You should see it as an opportunity to address a particular problem now rather than learning from a mistake at a later stage. In other words, look at any objections, turn them over in your mind, act on them if necessary and then move forward.

Not Everyone Will Get Your Vision

It's important to keep things in perspective. Yes, listen to the views of others, but ultimately you should be making your own decisions. Above all, don't let negative comments tunnel into your subconscious and undermine your confidence. Remember – and this is crucial – not everyone will get your vision. Actually, it goes deeper than that. No one – and I mean absolutely no one – will understand your vision better than you. Ultimately, you have to have faith in your own judgement.

This is something that will become apparent, as at every s\
your entrepreneurial career you'll make decisions based on\
intimate knowledge of the business. Inevitably, some of these de\
sions will be questioned by staff, investors or even your romanti\
partner. Again, you should listen to what others have to say, while
also bearing in mind that they (probably) don't see the whole
picture.

Maybe you've experienced this from the other side of the fence.
If you've worked for any length of time as an employee, you will
probably have encountered management decisions that make no
sense to you. Maybe they make life harder by introducing a new
process, or require you to change working hours. It might seem
pointless, but the manager – drawing on a comprehensive view of
the situation that employees don't have – will (usually) be doing it
for a good reason. They face criticism, but they stick to their plan.
So should you.

It's important not to take criticism personally. Naysayers, for the
most part, aren't trying to pick a fight or spoil your day, and nor are
they necessarily wrong in what they say. They just have a different
perspective. As US preacher T. D. Jakes has pointed out, the world
is inhabited by myriad creatures who each have their own world
view. While turtles feed on the ground, giraffes eat leaves high in
the trees. Consequently, they see the world differently.

Jakes's point is that the giraffes should not condemn the turtles,
but nor should they be swayed by their world view. 'Just because
turtles dwell at your feet doesn't mean you should come down from
your height and barter with, debate, or eat alongside them,' he says
in his book *Instinct: The Power to Unleash Your Inborn Drive*.

Just one last point on this topic. Seeking advice from experts in
the field will help you to validate your business concept, gain confidence and avoid getting too caught up in – or depressed by – the
views of naysayers. Once you know you're on the right track, criticism becomes easier to deal with.

Why Are You Doing This?

Validating an idea is important, but it only takes you part of the way towards creating a business that will thrive. Arguably, it is much more important to look at your plans and ask yourself what the *purpose* of your venture is. Why should it exist?

The importance of having a 'why' has perhaps been best articulated by Simon Sinek's book *Start with Why*. As he points out, when you look at an organization – small or large – the owners and employees will be fully aware of what the company does and how it does it. For instance: 'We make widgets and use machines to do it.' But the same managers and employees may be less clear if asked to explain *why* the business does what it does.

In terms of the branding and positioning of a business, purpose – the 'why' – is hugely important. Apple doesn't just make computers and phones; it makes machines that are a joy to use, and thus encourage their owners to maximize their creativity and productivity. And because people love using iPhones, Macs and iPads, they sell at premium prices. The above-market-average sale price is a result of the business finding and delivering on its 'why'.

Sometimes there's a social purpose as well. For instance, a fair-trade coffee company is not just in the business of shifting large numbers of product units. Their purpose is to sell great coffee while also making sure the producers on the ground get paid a decent amount of money. This purpose fuels demand, which in turn generates profit.

As Sinek sees it, the world's most inspirational business leaders – and this could apply to a first-time entrepreneur running a three-person team, or a CEO presiding over a multinational operation – are usually those who are absolutely clear about the purpose of their venture. Equally, they are more than capable of communicating the 'why' to staff, customers, suppliers and stakeholders. And, more fundamentally, knowing what you stand for will help you to become a better entrepreneur.

Here's a newsflash: running a business is probably going to be the hardest thing you ever do. Before you've set out on the entrepreneurial road, nothing can really prepare you for what lies ahead. It's a bit like raising a family. You have an idea of what it might be like, but until your children are born and begin to make their way down the road that leads from toddler to teenager and beyond, you can't really conceive of just how stressful those years will be. But you know you've got a reason – namely, to raise happy, balanced, successful children who make the most of their lives. That purpose keeps you going. Ultimately, the rewards are immeasurable.

It's the same thing when you're running a company. The thing that will help you weather the inevitable difficulties that arise is having a clear understanding of what you want to achieve.

What Is Purpose?

So what is 'purpose' in this context? How is it defined? Well, you can think about it as a distillation of a number of things: passion, values (both your personal values and those of the business), talents and skills.

Your passion will (or should) have a role in defining the kind of business you want to run. Now, this can mean many things. Some people have a passion for business itself – they love making deals, building a team, creating something from nothing – and the type of business may be secondary. Others are passionate about technology, so they are drawn to the digital sector. A music lover might start a record label or become a publicist for rising stars. Many people are keen to make a societal difference or create a greener planet, so they are drawn to businesses that aim to deliver those desired outcomes. This could mean anything from starting a vegan sandwich bar to developing technology that delivers clean water to drought-hit regions.

It's important to make a distinction here between the kind of long-term passion – or commitment – that will drive action, and a more fleeting enthusiasm. You might see something on the news – perhaps a report about an injustice – that fires you up and gets you shouting at the screen. But that's not the same as the kind of lasting passion that will see you working to address that injustice. You might feel strongly about climate change and the state of the planet. But in business terms what really matters is not just what you feel, but whether or not that feeling drives action.

Then there are your values, which will often define what you are comfortable doing and what you would rather avoid. This is about more than personal morality – for instance, avoiding certain industries for ethical reasons; it is also about the kind of person (and entrepreneur) you want to be. Essentially, values are the fundamental beliefs that underpin our motivations and thus (again) our actions.

Consider the example of Helen Tupper and Sarah Ellis, who both enjoyed success on the corporate ladder before going into business together as co-founders of their coaching company, Amazing If. Drawing on their own experiences, their purpose is to help individuals get the most out of 'squiggly' careers. What is a squiggly career, you ask? Well, essentially we're talking about the kind of working trajectory that doesn't develop in a linear way – say, from fresh new employee to eventual seat on the board – but rather takes a (potentially more interesting) course that involves taking charge of a diverse range of projects or transitioning to different roles within an organization.

As Sarah explains, she and Helen work well together because they share common values: 'We are both different as people, but our values are the same. We are both very achievement-oriented and we care about developing people.' Those values map neatly on to the purpose of Amazing If.

Values might also determine the scale of your business. Yvette Noel-Schure is a veteran music-industry publicist who worked for many years at Sony Music before setting up her own business. Today, she represents major music stars such as Beyoncé and Buju Banton. She is an in-demand publicist, but importantly she has made the decision to work only with people that she feels aligned with.

'I go in hard for my clients and I want to know what they are giving back to the world,' she says. 'I won't give time to people whose views clash with mine.' Consequently, she has made a decision that Schure Media Group should be a boutique operation rather than a business that grows into an industry giant.

Lastly, there are your talents and your skills. These are the personal attributes that will play an important role in shaping the purpose and direction of your business. They are part of the toolkit that we rely on when building a business.

Your Reason for Being

The question is, how do these elements blend into a clear – and clarity is hugely important – purpose?

Well, the first step is to ask yourself the following questions:

- What are you really setting out to achieve with this venture? Or, to put it another way, what do you want from it?
- How will it make your life better and more satisfying in terms of your passions and values?

It might be helpful to see this through the prism of a Japanese concept known as *Ikigai*. To put a complex philosophy as simply as possible, your *Ikigai* is your reason for being. It's the direction and purpose that make your life worthwhile and give it meaning.

Now, finding your purpose isn't necessarily an easy or simple exercise. For one thing, as we progress through life, there are always going to be people who (often for the best possible reasons) will try to define our purpose for us – for example, the parent who is determined that their children go into medicine or law when their ambitions actually extend in other directions. Sometimes, it can be hard not to be swayed by what other people expect. And even if

IKIGAI

A Japanese concept meaning 'a reason for being'

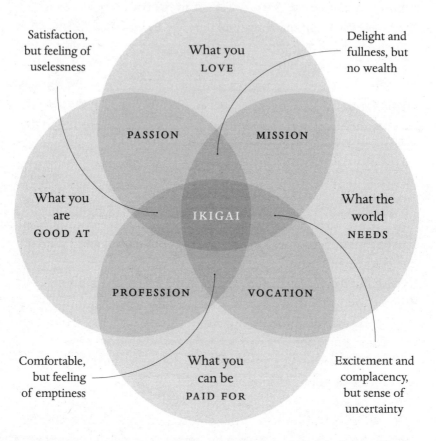

Satisfaction,
but feeling of
uselessness

What you
LOVE

Delight and
fullness, but
no wealth

PASSION

MISSION

What you
are
GOOD AT

IKIGAI

What the
world
NEEDS

PROFESSION

VOCATION

Comfortable,
but feeling
of emptiness

What you
can be
PAID FOR

Excitement and
complacency,
but sense of
uncertainty

there are no external pressures, very often we struggle to know our-selves. Maybe it's something we don't give enough thought to.

So, before you start a business, take some time to think about what you want:

- What makes you come alive?
- What inspires you?
- What are you passionate about?

Then think about your strengths, skills and talents. Some of them are innate – they just seem to come naturally – and others are learned. Consider all your talents and select a top three for special attention. We all enjoy doing what we're good at. If your strengths align with the requirements of your business, that's a good sign.

Adding Value

You should think about how you add value in a situation. This ties in with your strengths and your specific skills and experience. Will you be able to use these to their best effect in your chosen business? For instance, if you plan to start a training consultancy, what are you bringing to the table that will add real value for clients? If you plan to start a cafe on a high street where there are already two others, where can you add value and differentiate your business? This could come down to the warmth of your personality, your culinary skills or a vision to create a real community hub.

And finally, how do you measure success in your life? Imagine looking back – hopefully from the perspective of a ripe old age. Have you fulfilled your life goals?

Defining Success

That last point leads us into an area that some people spend a lot of time thinking about and others barely consider – namely, what are you going to leave behind as a legacy when your life comes to an end? You could also see this as a way of defining what success (and a successful life) looks like.

On the business side, does success equate with the life-changing, multimillion-pound exit deal that we discussed earlier, or with the creation of a company that can be passed down to the next generation? And then there is lifestyle . . . Does success mean retiring at the age of forty and pursuing non-commercial hobbies, interests or passions? Or is the idea to take the money you've earned and move on to other interesting projects, perhaps in other sectors? Is philanthropy part of your thinking, or becoming an educator who nurtures up-and-coming talent?

Stepping back to look at the bigger picture, what kind of dent would you like to leave on the planet, and how do you want to be remembered by those who succeed you?

Now, you can perhaps overthink this a little. Truth be told, few people are remembered beyond three generations – but by thinking about your legacy, you are also focusing on your ideal life and your ideal business.

Changing Tack

At this point, it's worth acknowledging that life doesn't always go according to plan. You may be running a business – but, as it turns out, it isn't your ideal venture. It isn't quite what you thought it would be in terms of its potential and the life that it's delivering for you. In fact, you're beginning to ask, is it really worth it?

Everyone probably hits this particular wall at some stage – particularly on those days when everything seems to be a struggle. Which is fair enough, but if you find yourself repeatedly asking whether or not you want to carry on doing what you're doing, it's probably time for a change.

Ideally, that change shouldn't see you quitting company ownership for the security of a nine-to-five career. You are an entrepreneur, after all, and the desire to create something great runs in your blood. So what you may need to do is either change your business or start a new one.

The strategy will depend on the circumstances. If you're running a successful business that just doesn't sit right with you, you can always sell it and use the proceeds to kick-start a venture that you really believe in. Alternatively, you could change the business itself.

Let's say you run an architecture practice – one that was set up with the express purpose of working on interesting projects. In reality, in order to pay the bills, you've found yourself mostly working on fairly basic house extensions. You'll need to make a plan to win more interesting work, and where necessary cut back on the bread-and-butter jobs. Make time and create the financial headroom to go for the prestige projects – the ones that stretch and inspire you.

Making the switch from something that's just OK to a project that you really believe in can be transformative. Byron and I witnessed this recently through the experience of one of our mentees. She is now running an absolutely life-changing business. But in order to do that, she had to move on from her existing venture.

It is possible to get trapped, either as a result of financial obligations or because you have a contract. The latter is common when businesses are sold and the founder is obliged to stay on for an earn-out period. Some enjoy the role of stewardship; others would rather be moving on to something else. It is, however, a temporary situation. There is no reason not to make plans for the future.

Get Big or Stay Lean

One of the attractions of starting a company is that you can essentially create something that fits around your desired lifestyle.

Take your working environment. Depending on your business, it's quite possible to run a company from the comfort of your own home. Indeed, one of the by-products of the Covid-19 pandemic was to demonstrate that even very large businesses could operate quite successfully with most members of staff working remotely and meetings taking place via digital video-conferencing platforms such as Zoom or on the phone.

Indeed, there has been something of a cultural change. As the lockdown began to lift, it became apparent that large swathes of the workforce were not rushing back to the office. Some companies – notably Google and Facebook – extended home working. Others adopted a hybrid approach, with teams splitting their time between home and office. In some respects, this is good news for entrepreneurs who would rather work – mostly – from houses or apartments. It has become something that you can do simply. You can even (as Byron and I have chosen to do during the pandemic) become a 'digital nomad' and work from abroad.

Working from home isn't for everyone – some prefer office life – but you don't necessarily need to have thousands of square feet of space in a city-centre location to feel that you've made it. Sometimes, the best solution is to have a relatively small headquarters and just a few members of staff.

That's the route that we have taken – although it took a while to arrive at that point. When I started out in business, I had a vision of a big office with loads of staff, and it certainly began that way; but then I reflected on what we wanted and realized that we want to be lean. We don't want to have a lot of people to manage. That wouldn't align with the lifestyle that we want.

You might ask, why not? After all, the prestigious office is often thought of as one of the key indicators of success. It's a part of the dream. Well, we used to have offices in Croydon, Edgware and Blackpool, but we chose to strip it back and keep staff to a minimum. And frankly, it suits us. Dealing with lots of members of staff can be stressful, as can all the associated admin and regulatory issues – such as providing the right number of men's and women's toilets in the office. Staff and people can often mean dealing with some fairly petty issues.

It's not that we seek to avoid stress. We know that's a normal part of business. Rather, it's a case of apportioning the stress to where you want it to be, and avoiding the stress that you really don't want. Which may indeed be another factor in determining whether a particular business is right for you. If you don't like cold-call selling, then a business that will require you to do just that, day in, day out, is probably not optimal – unless, of course, you can find a partner who will handle that side of things for you. Likewise, if dealing with a constantly changing regulatory landscape is not your idea of fun, then it's probably not a good idea to go into an arena such as financial services, where there is not only a lot of bureaucracy but also some pretty hefty fines for non-compliance.

The truth is, we all get stressed by different things. Byron ran a property business that had a gas maintenance service in its portfolio. It was, as he freely acknowledges, something that he couldn't handle. The possibility of something going wrong – perhaps even resulting in a gas explosion – was a constant worry.

There was, however, a simple solution – namely, getting out of that side of the business. The moral? Figure out the stresses you are willing to accept, and think about your long-term vision and what you need to do to make your business a success based on *your* definition of success.

When Do You Have Enough?

Every decision you make about your business will have financial implications. For instance, if you decide to keep things small, that will potentially stunt your ability to grow, which will in turn impact on sales.

That's not necessarily a bad thing. As Paul Jarvis points out, measuring success purely in terms of how fast your revenues are growing can be deceptive: 'You could be earning a million dollars a year. But if it's costing you $999,950 to generate those sales figures, you're actually not doing very well.'

His solution with Fathom has been to concentrate on 'making customers very happy' rather than going all out to win new business. Ironically, this does deliver growth, as satisfied customers stay loyal and make recommendations.

You do, of course, have to be sure that what you're doing is sustainable – or, to put it another way, that the profits generated by the business are sufficient. Jarvis's philosophy is to ensure that he has enough to sustain his desired lifestyle. 'But you do have to check in on that,' he says. 'What is enough today may not be enough when you have children or buy a new house.'

'Are you crazy?'

Maybe someone questioned you when you announced your plans to leave a comfortable career and branch out on your own. And maybe you responded by asking yourself: 'Am I crazy? Is this the right thing to do?'

You're not crazy. But starting a business is a big step, and success isn't going to happen overnight. It may well be tough, but achieving your ambitions will be easier when you know your purpose.

After that, it's time to set some solid goals.

Chapter Two

Identify Your Goals

'The trouble with not having a goal is that you can spend
your life running up and down the field and never score.'

– Bill Copeland

Most of us know that it's important to set goals in order to achieve great things. We know that failing to plan is planning to fail. And we know that in order to arrive at a destination, we need to understand how we intend to get there.

So why is it that so many people – including those who are extremely talented and bursting with great ideas – fail to fully realize their ambitions?

Well, one key factor is flawed goal setting. It's all too easy to trick yourself into thinking that you've set out a series of clear objectives – knowing that this is a vital part of any life or business plan – when all you have really done is jot down some vague wishes or fuzzy aspirations.

Is that such a bad thing? The short answer is 'yes'. If you want to succeed in just about any aspect of life, you really have to understand the process of effective goal setting and why it works. Equally, you also need to know why so many people fail to achieve their objectives.

So, let's start by looking at an example of what not to do. It's 1 January and you've decided that this is the year that fitness will become a priority. You pick up your phone and type a New Year's resolution into a note-taking app: 'This year I will get fit.' A simple, clear goal.

Actually, it's not. The problem here is that without any clear and actionable objectives and definitions, you don't really have a goal. For one thing, you haven't specified what 'fit' means. Are you thinking in terms of running a half-marathon by autumn, or do you see fitness in terms of being able to run a few hundred yards to the bus stop without becoming breathless? Or is it all about losing weight and feeling a bit more toned?

And how do you propose to get 'fit'? What steps are you going to take to ensure that you move from where you are now to where you want to be? Unless you know this, it's unlikely that you will succeed. Instead, the New Year's resolution will be quietly forgotten by as early as mid-January.

The same principle applies to other common aspirations, such as 'This year I will start a business' or 'I will be rich in five years' time'.

Goal setting is an underrated and incredibly powerful tool. It will help you to do more, achieve more and be more. Whatever you are seeking to achieve, you should be continuously setting goals, working towards them and measuring your progress.

But what does that mean in practice? What does effective goal setting look like?

Be Audacious – Aim for the Stars

Whatever your objective, it makes sense to think big – or, to put it another way, you should always reach for outcomes that might initially seem to be beyond your grasp. As the great Michelangelo is believed to have once said, 'The greater danger for most of us is not that our aim is too high and we miss it, but that it is too low and we reach it.'

Let me give you an example. Type the words 'goal setting' into Google, and one of the first things that you're likely to come across is the acronym SMART. Broken down, it stands for:

S – Specific
M – Measurable
A – Attainable
R – Realistic
T – Time-defined

This is undoubtedly a neat acronym, as it provides a simple method of remembering a goal-setting formula. And it's doubly neat because we all like to be smart. But it's also a formula that encourages you to be realistic. While that may sound eminently sensible, in practical terms being overly cautious can very often be counterproductive.

Think of it this way. Say one of your goals is to run a sole-trader business that turns over £100,000 in its first year. A business adviser might look at that, frown and say: 'You know what, £30,000 would be more realistic, given that you're starting from scratch.'

So this is what happens . . . You aim for £30,000 because that's what you think you'll be able to achieve. The problem is that if your aim falls short, you perhaps earn £20,000 – and at that level, your business is actually unsustainable.

But aim for £100,000 and your ambitions are automatically set higher. Even if you only hit half that figure, you're still doing OK.

You can apply the same principle to disposable income. If your goal is to take £50,000 a year out of the business as income and you fall short by a few thousand, there's no harm done. But aim for a more 'realistic' £20,000, and any shortfall means that you can't pay your rent or mortgage.

Aiming high can feel uncomfortable. You may, for example, think that by lowering your personal bar to a 'realistic' level you are more likely to succeed. But often the opposite is true. By setting your sights low, there is a real chance that you will simply fail more quickly. So, get comfortable with being uncomfortable. Conquer any doubts you have and go for what Bianca often refers to as the 'big, hairy, audacious goals'.

We're not just talking about financial and business matters here. When Bianca was at school – and this is something she remembers very well – a teacher told her that she should aim for a B in maths. In his view, he was probably setting a realistic target. Fortunately, Bianca's father made a simple but hugely important point: 'Why would anyone aim for a B in anything?' And he was right. Go for a B, have a bad day in the exam room and you get a C. Aim for an A* and even if you miss it, you still get a good grade.

Neither Bianca nor I are urging you to strive for the impossible. Some outcomes may be beyond your reach, particularly those that try to defy the laws of physics, chemistry or biology. But if you have a vision, don't listen to those who tell you it's impossible or unrealistic. The Wright brothers were probably told by all and sundry that man was not capable of flying. I imagine they were hearing that right up to the point when their plane took to the air. Thomas Edison would have experienced a huge amount of scepticism just before he developed sound recording, long-distance communication and electricity generation. Marie Van Brittan Brown, a nurse, likely wouldn't have been expected to create and patent the two-way microphone and camera security system that led to what we now call CCTV. There were probably a lot of people who cautioned Richard Branson that starting an airline was not a great idea for someone whose expertise was in the music industry. The list goes on.

A Good Goal

So, with 'realism' set to one side, what should a goal look like? Well, with the 'R' removed, the acronym SMAT doesn't look quite so neat, so let's leave that behind and say that a goal should be:

- Clear
- Specific
- Measurable / deadline-defined

Clarity of purpose is essential. For instance, if you already run a business, it's not enough to simply say, 'I want it to perform better this year than it did in the previous twelve months.' To be anything more than an aspiration, it's important to pin down what that actually means. You could, for example, put a number on it. If turnover was £250,000 last year, you could define 'better' as £300,000 or £350,000.

Do the same for personal goals. Rather than saying, 'My goal this year is to buy a new car,' specify the make, model, year, price and trim. In the case of a new house, think about location, type (detached, semi, terrace), number of rooms and size of the garden. As you add the detail, something that was vague and generalized is thrown into sharp relief.

Get the Specs Right

How do you judge if the goal you've set is sufficiently clear and specific?

Here's a useful thought experiment: imagine that you are sending details of your goal to a factory where it is to be manufactured. The specs need to be precise enough for the manufacturer to send it back fully complete and ready. The logic is this – if all you send to your manufacturer is a generic description of a car, what you get back could be anything from a Ford Ka to an Aston Martin. More likely, the manufacturer will say, 'I can't work with this.' But provide a detailed description and you'll get exactly what you asked for.

The more specific the goal is, the more measurable it becomes. And that's important. It's perhaps too easy to trick ourselves into thinking we've achieved an objective when we actually haven't done anything of the sort. Let's return to that goal of improving business performance. Maybe turnover rises by £3,000 against the previous year. You could tell yourself that performance has improved, even though competition has eaten into your margins and profits are down. But if a figure for desired turnover has been named, alongside a target for profits, then there are no grey areas. The goal has either been achieved or it hasn't.

You should keep your measures pretty simple, though. A smart six-year-old should be able to look at your goal and tell you in an instant whether or not you've done what you said you would.

And finally, the goal should be attached to a timeline. You're going to buy the car you've specified by the end of the year. Or, to get fit, you have six months to turn flat turnover into an upward curve. Three months to make the transition from couch potato to someone who can easily run five kilometres.

This is an important discipline. The deadline may slip, but every time you hit a milestone date on the calendar, you have no choice but to look at your progress so far. And if the timetable is slipping, you have to think about why, and how you can get things back on course.

So, you now know what a goal looks like. This is the point where things begin to get both a little more complicated and a lot more interesting. In the next section, I'm going to take an in-depth and very practical look at the process of setting not just one but multiple goals.

The Power of Paper

The good news is that you don't need to rush out and buy expensive software or even download an app for your phone or tablet. In fact, you should definitely leave the tech locked away in a drawer for a while. The only tools required here are a pen and multiple sheets of paper. Writing your goals down is – and I can't stress this enough – the most effective way of ensuring that they are acted upon.

There's a good reason for this. Writing – the very tangible act of picking up a pen and making a mark on a piece of paper – engages the brain in a way that tapping out a few words on a keyboard never can.

For one thing, writing is a complex skill. It's an activity that requires significant coordination between body and brain. It requires effort. Thus, what you write down leaves a deeper impression on your subconscious mind than anything you type out.

There's an emotional factor as well. Imagine for a moment that you've just received a letter from a friend – someone you haven't seen in a long time. If it arrives in email format, it will doubtless be interesting, funny, informative and perhaps intimate. But let's imagine that it has been posted to you and written in longhand. This version will have all of the attributes above, but it will also be more personal. You'll get a sense of the craft and commitment that went into it.

The same is true when you write down your goals and ambitions. You're making an emotional statement to yourself, and a commitment that is likely to stick in your mind.

And, stylistically speaking, the goals will be more personal to you. Your handwriting, your annotations, your own way of laying out the page. You are expressing yourself.

Success Rates

Writing your goals down on paper is more than just a nicety. A study by Gail Matthews of the Dominican University of California found that those who write their goals down are 42 per cent more likely to achieve them. A Harvard Business School study came up with similar findings: while only 3 per cent of people bother to write down their goals, they are, on average, three times more successful in terms of achievement and fulfilment than the 13 per cent who set themselves objectives but don't commit them to paper.

So, before you do anything further, buy yourself a notebook (or several!) or find some sheets of paper. We are now going to map out your goals together.

Step One – The Top Three

Try this simple exercise. Taking no more than sixty seconds – and without thinking too much about it – write down your three most important goals. Just three – that's all you'll need at this stage.

1.

2.

3.

Because you haven't overthought it, the chances are that you have just committed to paper the three most important objectives in your life. This exercise is useful because it provides an insight into your priorities across both your personal and your working life. It will help point you in your direction of travel, before you begin to set out plans in more detail.

Step Two – Your Starter for Ten

Now the real work begins. At this point, I would suggest you find a place in your home where there is plenty of room and you won't be disturbed. The space is important. It could be a large desk, or better still – and this is what I gravitate towards – a patch of floor where you can lay out the individual pieces of paper that you're going to use.

And there will be a lot of them. You're going to write down not three but *ten* major goals, with a single piece of paper allocated to each.

At first, this might seem a bit daunting. Even if you include the three goals that you thought of initially – and it's probable that you will – coming up with ten might be a big ask. So my advice is to break your objectives down into important categories. For example:

- Income
- Net worth/assets
- Business
- Family and relationships
- Health
- Lifestyle

There are good reasons for this. For one thing, you'll no longer be looking at a vast empty plain of possibilities that you are struggling to fill with goals. Instead, you have categories covering important areas in your personal and your working life. These provide structure for your goal setting.

The relationship between these categories also provides useful guidance. No one lives out their existence entirely at the office. Our working lives are interconnected with home, family and circles of friends and associates. By using this model, goal setting becomes holistic and reflects the fact that our personal and public ambitions cannot be separated. We want to do well in business or in our careers because we also want to live in nice homes, have healthy and productive family relationships and enjoy stimulating leisure time. It's all part of a matrix.

I should stress here that it's up to you to decide how much weight to place on each of these categories. In some cases, most of your goals could be categorized in terms of income – which, in turn, may relate directly to work success or starting a business – because that's where your ambitions currently lie. But keep all of the categories in mind as you develop your plans. You might find, for example, that you have six income goals, two business objectives, and one each for family and health.

This is only a start. Over time, those ten goals should turn into a hundred. Goal setting is an ongoing process.

Step Three – Add the Detail

As you sit on the floor surrounded by pieces of paper, the first thing you'll notice is that you have a lot of white space to fill. That's not only fine, it's essential. To make your goals meaningful – or 'specific' – it's important to put in as much detail as possible.

Write down everything you can think of about the goal you want to achieve. Maybe the uppermost objective in your mind is to move from the house that you're living in now to something bigger – perhaps even palatial. That's fine. On that piece of paper, write down every detail of your dream property.

Step Four – Set a Deadline

Once you've filled in the detail, put a deadline on each of your goals, stating when you want to achieve your objective by. Each goal will have its own timeline, but typically you'll find yourself planning for periods ranging from a few months to a few years. This will provide a time management framework, and a means to measure your actual progress against your original plan.

Step Five – Identify the Obstacles

You may need a new sheet of paper for this next part . . .

So, you know where you're going and when you want to get there. Now you need to look at any factors that could stop you in your tracks. Let's say you want a house in the Bahamas. How much do you know about the practicalities of buying a property in such a far-off place? Do you know how easy (or difficult) it is for someone not born on the islands to buy a house there? Have you considered the visa rules? How much will the property cost and how will you raise the money? Is this a retirement home or will you need (or want) to go on working while you're living there, and what are the implications of that?

A long list of obstacles should not be a deterrent. Once you've taken a cool-headed look at the hurdles that lie ahead of you, you can work out how to overcome them.

Step Six – Setting Sub-Goals

As you address obstacles and issues, a logical next step is to create sub-goals. These are the smaller, tactical objectives that will enable you to achieve those ten goals that you have committed to paper. Often these will be directly associated with overcoming obstacles, addressing tricky issues or simply putting in place some of the essential elements of the plan. For instance, if a house in the Bahamas is in your sights, you can create a series of goals linked to ensuring that you have the money available to complete the purchase.

Step Seven – Identifying What You Need to Succeed

A key element of any goal-based plan is an understanding of the attributes and/or assets that will enable you to reach your objective as quickly as possible. The assets are usually easy to identify: a writer needs a laptop; a retailer requires a shop space, an e-commerce website or both; a driving instructor must possess or have access to a dual-control car.

But there are less tangible things to consider, not least the skills and knowledge (and in some cases, the qualifications) required to bring an ambition to fruition – or indeed, to deliver on the various tactical elements of the goals along the way. Think carefully about these factors. If the end goal is to establish, say, an accountancy business, there are some obvious steps to take in terms of researching the qualifications, required experience and membership of a professional body that will ensure the venture is compliant with current regulations while also establishing its credibility in the eyes of potential customers. However, beyond the purely professional side of things, there are other skills to consider. These include marketing (how you find your customers), people management (keeping clients and employees on board) and networking. So, what are you good at, what are you qualified to do, where do the gaps lie and how do you fill them?

Personal ambitions require similar attention to detail. Maybe you've just bought a new home and your goal is to turn a rear plot that is currently a building site into a mature and beautiful garden within two summers. That will require both knowledge (of local soils, appropriate plants, etc.) and skills (such as design and construction techniques).

Step Eight – Identify the People

The likelihood is that you will also need people to help you. What that means in practice will depend on your goals. If you're creating a garden – complete with hard landscaping – you'll probably benefit from some expert horticultural advice, and you might require the services of a professional gardener. If you're branching out on your own to start a small service company, then the first thing you'll probably be thinking about is how to identify the right people who have the appropriate skills so you can create your team. If you're setting up a business, you may wish to find a business mentor or coach to help you get started and prevent costly mistakes. You could equally be identifying advisers, investors, non-executive directors, friends that can offer advice, or well-connected people who can help you tap into their own networks and even assist you with a referral for your first client. We'll consider this in more detail in Chapter Six, where we'll look at your personal boardroom, stakeholder matrix and the needs in your business.

Time to Turn Your Goals into a Plan

At this point, as you look at the goals you've created, it might seem like most of the hard planning work has been completed. Actually, there's a lot more to do. It's certainly true to say that in setting goals you've created the core of a plan. There is, however, an element of the route map to success that is missing: the actions that will turn your objectives into realities.

A plan requires a sequence. It would be impossible to act on all your goals and sub-goals at once. That would simply pull you in a lot of different directions, rather than propelling you forward.

So the key is to prioritize. Study your goals and decide which are the most important at any particular time. Dig deeper into the obstacles, and take a view on which solutions and sub-goals are most likely to move you towards your stated objective at the most rapid rate possible.

The 80/20 Rule

A useful tool to deploy here is the 80/20 rule, also known as the Pareto principle after Vilfredo Pareto, a nineteenth-century Italian economist. The principle is this: 80 per cent of output comes from 20 per cent of input. Essentially, it's talking about time management, and underlying the formula is the simple concept that spreading yourself too thinly is a really bad idea.

In my experience, that is absolutely right. Let's say your goal is to increase sales and you have one hundred customers on your books. As the 80/20 rule indicates, 80 per cent of your sales are going to come from 20 per cent of your customers. By focusing fully on the twenty customers who are most likely to increase their purchases, you therefore generate far better results than if you spend your time arranging meetings with the other eighty. Concentrating your efforts on the activities that are most likely to produce results represents the best possible use of your time.

Rewiring Your Brain

How real are your dreams? By this stage, they should certainly feel real to you, because you've thought everything through in a great deal of detail.

And this is important. In my experience, the more real a goal seems to you, the more likely you are to see it make the transition from an abstract thought or concept into something that is a tangible part of your world. That's true of anything from getting yourself fit enough to run a marathon through to launching an ambitious business.

You begin to build in the sense of reality as soon as you start writing down your goals. The simplest and most effective way to do this is to write down each of your objectives as if it has already been achieved, and to write in the first person, starting each sentence with 'I'. So, instead of 'I intend to run a half-marathon', write 'I have run a half-marathon'.

What you're really doing here is rewiring your thought processes. If you say you are *going* to do something (future tense), you are telling your brain that it's an option – an outcome that might at some point happen. But if you write 'I have started a business', at a subconscious level that becomes your reality.

Visualizing Your Goal

Let's take this concept a bit further. Each goal that you've defined should not only be attainable, it should also *feel* attainable. Psychologically speaking, it should be part of your mental landscape before it becomes a part of your life. The goals you've written down provide a foundation, but as you begin to put your plans into action, another tool can be brought into play: visualization.

Think of it this way – you haven't, as yet, bought your house in the Bahamas, but you can see it in your mind's eye and have begun to feel what it would be like to own it. Visualizing your goal or objective generates an emotional connection. It creates an internal driver that pushes you towards achievement.

Does that sound a little New Age? Well, consider this. Let's assume for a moment that one of your goals is a Jaguar F-Type coupe – I'll leave it to you to add your own colour, trim and features. Maybe you've seen one in a magazine. Maybe a friend owns one. Or perhaps you've seen more than one overtake you in the fast lane. For whatever reason, the psychographic stars are in alignment. This car is the perfect fit for you.

So far, you've made that judgement from a distance. But why not cement the bond? Visit a showroom. Book a test drive. Get a sense of what it feels like to take the car out on the road. And when you do, here's what happens: as you put the car into top gear, your endorphins start to flow. You have made an emotional connection – one that will provide a psychological support structure as you deal with all the practical issues that stand between you and the day you pick up the logbook. In your mind's eye, that car is already yours. Now all you have to do is put your plan into operation.

Another tip – and this applies to goals that are physical objects – is to keep a record on your phone or tablet. Take a picture of that Jaguar and put it as your wallpaper or lock screen. OK, so maybe at the moment you have a picture of your partner or children looking back at you whenever you reach for your phone, but they know you love them. They won't be offended if you replace them with a picture of a Jag – for a while, at least. And they'll be really pleased on the day you drive it home.

The same is true of property-related goals. When Bianca and I discovered that we had a common goal of moving to a new and better house, we compared notes and found that our visions were remarkably similar. We both wanted a double-fronted property with five bedrooms, a substantial garden front and back, and a pool.

So, we set out our goal using the steps described above. In addition to visualizing the house, we went house hunting. We began to build a sense of what living in our dream home would actually be like. We made a connection between what we were planning and the physical reality of the kind of home we wanted, without yet knowing how we would make it happen. We purchased our new home within six months.

The Learning Curve

Goal setting is ongoing – you should never stop doing it. And as you review your progress, it will probably also become apparent that there is a lot to learn. The goals you wrote down with pen and paper during that first exercise will – hopefully – soon bear some fruit in terms of actual achievement and attainment. But maybe there are gaps in your plan. Things that you missed – or didn't think about – the first time around.

For instance, when Bianca launched her hosiery business – Bianca Miller London – the concept was an inclusive 'nude' hosiery brand for people of all skin tones. It was both a business opportunity and a mission. The *Oxford English Dictionary* entry for 'nude' defines the colour as 'pinkish beige' – not a colour that applies to the skin tones of the majority of the world's population.

So, Bianca set herself a number of clear goals:

- The brand would be inclusive, providing products for a broad range of skin tones.
- The products would be manufactured in Britain.
- They would be available on the high street.

All went according to plan. Bianca worked with Pantone on the colours and then looked around until she found a company that could offer manufacturing in the UK. Once it was up and running, she succeeded in getting Bianca Miller London products into major retail chains such as Selfridges and Topshop.

Job done, then? Well, not quite, because there was more goal setting and planning to do. As Bianca acknowledges, the initial planning hadn't really touched on the financial performance of the company in the longer term. Ideally, the financial goals should have been set right at the beginning, along with the 'vanity' goals.

In business, there is always more to do. It is necessary to continually reassess your objectives. You might not get everything right first time, but when you see the gaps, new goals can be factored in.

And here's the good news. Over time, goal setting becomes second nature, and you get better at doing it.

Reverse Engineering

What we've been talking about so far could be described as 'best practice'. You set out ten goals, and over time build that up to ninety or one hundred. You follow a tried-and-trusted process.

But you have to start somewhere, and before you sit down to write out your objectives, the beginning of your journey may be a simple idea that lodges itself in your mind. To turn that idea into practice you effectively reverse-engineer the goals that will guide you to your destination.

Let me give you an example. A few years ago, I bought a Range Rover from a man who had a driveway full of similar luxury vehicles, which he planned to either hang on to or sell. He had no real plan to do anything else with them. But I saw an opportunity. It occurred to me that all those cars could be deployed commercially, rather than sitting unused on a gravel parking area. More specifically, those cars were ideal luxury hires. They were the kind of vehicles that you might rent to take you and your friends to a wedding or another special event.

On a more personal note, I rather liked the idea of having access to a range of luxury vehicles which I would be able to drive. In other words, the potential was there for a commercial venture that would also be great fun to be involved with. I suggested this to the owner, and he replied that he wasn't interested.

But I persevered. I studied the market and found that most luxury private-hire businesses were fairly unprofessionally run. Often, everything was operated by a single individual taking bookings via a smartphone. They weren't quite cowboy businesses, but they weren't far off. So, I set out detailed goals for a really professional operation with a great website. The owner still resisted, so I started the business myself, and later on he bought shares. I saw the problem with the existing business model and, with great vision, I set the goals and made the cars – often considered an liability because they take money out of your pocket – into an income-producing asset and a business that added to my lifestyle.

Goal setting – as the basis of a meticulous planning process – had turned an idea into a living, breathing, successful business. And that's what I would like you to take away from this chapter. If you take the right approach to developing your goals, all things are possible.

> *'Vision without action is a daydream.*
> *Action without vision is a nightmare.'*
>
> – Japanese proverb

Chapter Three

Get Your Sh★t Together

'You have to eat the dream, you have to sleep the dream, you have to
dream the dream. You gotta touch [it], you have to see it when nobody
else sees it. You have to feel it when it's not tangible. You have to believe
it when you cannot see it. You gotta be possessed with the dream.'

– Eric Thomas

One of the world's leading motivational speakers and business consultants, Eric Thomas could probably have found half a dozen or
more reasons to lead a very different kind of life from the one he
enjoys today. At twelve years old, he discovered that the man who
had raised him was not, in fact, his real father. Feeling like everything he thought he knew had been turned upside down, he argued
with his family and the tensions became so intense that he ended up
homeless and living on the street. It could have been the start of a
downhill trajectory.

It wasn't. A preacher encouraged him to return to school.
Thomas studied hard and eventually went on to earn a PhD. A
lucrative career followed. So when he urges those with ideas and
ambitions to eat and sleep their dreams, his advice is more than theory. As his own story illustrates, success is often hard-won. Realizing
an ambition requires absolute commitment and focus.

There are many things that can divert you from your chosen
entrepreneurial path by feeding a nagging doubt about your ability
to succeed. You may have encountered personal difficulties in your
past. Your present circumstances might not be ideal. External factors such as a downturn in the economy could encourage you to
hold back on your plans until things improve.

Factors such as these create tension. On the one hand, you have a great business idea. On the other, you are looking at an array of obstacles, some of which seem insurmountable. There are two roads you can take. You can press ahead with your plans, or you can find reasons (excuses) to put your plans on hold.

Even once your business is up and running, you will continue to face similar challenges. A client cancels a contract. The landlord ups the rent. A pandemic locks down the economy. Events such as these are triggers. They require you to make choices. Sometimes, the choice is between finding solutions or giving up.

Which brings us back to what Eric Thomas says about realizing your dreams. To succeed, it is necessary to concentrate absolutely on what you want to achieve, rather than making excuses or finding reasons to fail. The key to doing this is a winning mindset that will enable you to get your sh*t together and stay on course, even in the face of adversity.

The Seeds of Failure

You might be asking why anyone would seek to make excuses and justify failure. Why would they knowingly undermine their own ambitions?

The answer is complicated. There are quite a few reasons why talented and visionary people effectively self-sabotage. Often, it's that they are hampered by fears and insecurities, which they may not consciously be aware of.

So, what are the most common fears that prevent entrepreneurs from pursuing or fulfilling their ambitions? You can actually assemble quite a lengthy list (some of which we will look at in more detail in the pages that follow), including:

- Fear of failure
- Fear of not being good enough
- Fear of being unworthy

- Fear of success
- Fear of greatness
- Fear of being judged by others
- Fear of having to work too hard

In addition, you could stir some excuses into the pot marked 'self-sabotage'. For instance, the feeling that others will hold you back, or the belief that it will be impossible to raise the money required to get your venture up and running.

Fear of Failure

One of the most common psychological traps is a fear of failure. This is often rooted in an overblown concern about what others think. When you work hard – and are seen to be doing so by those around you – you are making a very public statement. You are effectively saying: 'Look everyone, I'm really going for this.' But there is also the possibility that, despite all your hard work, you might not succeed. For some people, this leads to a fear of being identified as a failure.

This fear is insidious, because it's usually unconscious. You don't say to yourself, 'I fear failure, so I'll give up.' Instead, you find ways to block your own progress. Perhaps you do this by procrastinating. The business plan is always being written but is never completed. Plans are put on hold because the economic climate isn't right.

Fear of failure can also be based on previous experience – or, to be more precise, a failure that has occurred at some time in the past. Let's say you started a business, ran it for a few years, and either it never got off the ground or it thrived for a while and then something went wrong. Maybe you made some mistakes. Perhaps the market changed, or a better-funded competitor came in and hoovered up your market share. After all the early optimism, you had to admit that you tried your hardest but it wasn't good enough.

Does this stop you from trying again? It can, but it shouldn't.

The broad point here is that just because something doesn't work out today, it doesn't mean that anything attempted tomorrow will also fail.

Failure Is Feedback

It is vital to see failure as a chance to learn. As the Spanish philosopher George Santayana put it, 'Those who cannot remember the past are condemned to repeat it.' Acknowledging what you've got wrong and learning lessons from it are key to making progress. Here's how to look at mistakes positively.

Failure is feedback. It tells you what you've been doing wrong and (by extension) how you can set about putting things right the next time around. The mistakes you make today provide the information you'll need to succeed in the future.

Let's consider a couple of life examples. You've been doing well at school and then the mock exams roll around. You perform badly in two subjects and you face a choice. Do you – on the basis of the mock results – give up on those subjects, saying 'I'll never be any good at this'? Or do you look at the returned papers and teacher feedback and then address your weaknesses before the real exams? Clearly, the second option is the best one.

Now consider a business that was forced to close after running out of cash. It was a shock, as by one set of measures, everything had been going well. Sales were good and revenues grew as a result. The problem was that suppliers (and the landlord) were taking upfront payments, while customers had been given between one and three months to pay their invoices. This was fine at first, but after a few late payments and defaults, there wasn't enough cash in the bank to pay salaries. It was a problem the owner didn't see coming. But if they see their mistakes as a lesson, then next time round it will be different. Cash management will be top of the agenda. That is, of course, if the owner decides to start another venture.

There Is No Shame in Failing

Reaction to the failure of a business is in part cultural. Or, to put it another way, there are different attitudes to failure depending on where you happen to be located. In the US, entrepreneurs don't plan or want to fail but they realize that it's a possibility. And if it happens, they tend to move on to the next project. There is no shame in that. Indeed, it's expected that true entrepreneurs learn from their mistakes, lick their wounds and start again. All individuals are different, of course, but that tends to be the cultural norm in America.

The UK, in contrast, has traditionally been a bit different. In some quarters at least, the failure of a business is seen as a mark of shame – a stigma. Much of this is down to the reactions of others. If a business has to pull down the shutters, friends, acquaintances and even relatives are likely to say something along the lines of: 'That's a real shame – I guess you'll be getting a regular job now.' In the same situation, a typical US response would be: 'I'm sorry it didn't work out. What's your next venture?'

These are external responses, but they can get inside the brain of an entrepreneur and sow the seeds of self-doubt. You really have to change the conversation and view failure, and learning from it, as part of your development – and, actually, see it as an *essential* part of your development. As Robert Kiyosaki, author of the bestselling book *Rich Dad, Poor Dad* has pointed out, when people play it too safe, when they're afraid to ask for help and go for it – when they're afraid of failure – they are playing stupid by not playing the game.

Fear of Success

Sitting at the opposite end of the spectrum from fear of failure is fear of success – or indeed, fear of greatness. But why would you shy away from something that, nominally at least, everyone wants?

Well, there are reasons. You might feel that you're simply not good enough and will be discovered as an imposter. Or that you don't deserve success or indeed greatness. (We'll be covering these in depth in Chapter Five.) There may also be a concern that success will cut you off from the people you've grown up with. Or that friends or acquaintances will somehow like you less.

Let's say you work very hard, with an absolute laser focus on making your business a success. To those not directly involved in what you're doing, it might seem that you've changed. That you've become obsessed with money. Indeed, someone might even say to your face: 'It's all about the money with you, isn't it?' It isn't all about the money, of course – or it needn't be. People start businesses for all sorts of reasons. Some want to do good in the world, or they see a problem that they would like to solve. That is their purpose. But generating money is intrinsic to a sustainable, viable business.

So, being told that you've become money-obsessed could be something you have to deal with. But, actually, dealing with it isn't that difficult. Making money isn't something to be ashamed of. Quite the opposite, in fact. You can enjoy the money you make and take a great deal of satisfaction from the financial freedom you've attained, while at the same time being totally aware that you also have a purpose that is about much more than piling up cash in the bank.

Excuses, Excuses

It's all too easy to find excuses not to do something – especially if the something in question involves years of hard work and commitment. You might tell yourself that people are holding you back. Or that you're too young or too old to start a business. But these are nothing more than self-limiting beliefs.

Rather like the fear of failure or success, the rationalizations for not doing what it takes to build something great are often unconscious or disguised. And they are often characterized as unassailable facts.

Time Management

Take the simple statement 'I don't have enough time'. On the face of it, this might appear to be true. You've mapped out a route to launch a business, and there are a hundred and one things that must be done. Meanwhile, you're also working full-time as an employee for someone else. It's impossible, therefore, to tick off all the items on your extensive to-do list – finding partners, designing a website, sending a product spec to a factory in Asia.

But here's the thing. Other people have started businesses in exactly the same circumstances, and – guess what – everyone has exactly the same number of hours in the day.

So, stop thinking in terms of not having enough time. Instead, focus on scheduling the time you do have more effectively. That's what successful people do. They establish priorities, and make the 'power moves' that enable them to progress.

Turning 'I Can't' into 'I Can'

Another belief masquerading as fact can be characterized by the simple phrase 'I can't'.

The expression often goes hand in hand with a sense of being realistic or accepting that a situation can't be turned around. But realism is not necessarily a good thing, especially when it's actually a form of defeatism. As Will Smith once said: 'Being realistic is the quickest path to mediocrity.'

The truth is that a lot of situations *can* be turned around. Let me give an example. One of our mentees was due to meet a client, but the delivery of a new line of products was late. The mentee's first reaction was to call off the meeting on the basis that it was impossible to arrange a delivery on time. Our advice was to look at the alternatives, and they found an obvious solution – using existing samples to show the quality of the brand to the customer and build a rapport, prior to the finished product arriving.

In other words, you can turn 'I can't' into 'I can' by finding an alternative solution. The solution may not be perfect, but what really matters is that it gets the job done.

Self-Belief

Behind a great many entrepreneurs is a niggling fear that they themselves are not good enough to make their ideas work. This can easily become a self-fulfilling prophecy: tell yourself you can't hack it, and you probably won't.

So why might you think you're not up to the job? Well, you might think that you don't have the skills, experience or qualifications. But none of those factors represents a good reason for not pursuing your dream. If you need qualifications, sign up for classes and get them. If you lack experience in a certain industry, find a mentor or a consultant to help. If you feel something is lacking in your personal abilities, seek advice from a business or life coach. There are always solutions.

Beware of comparing yourself to others. No two people have exactly the same attributes, talents and experience. You might look at someone who's already working in your desired sector and think, 'I'm really not as good as that.' And nor will you be – if you let that feeling of inferiority deter you from pursuing your goal.

No one is born with skills and experience. We all get good (and better) at what we do by action and practice. And if we don't throw our hats into the ring, then we won't develop or grow. It's also worth remembering that you don't have to be amazing at absolutely everything. In some areas, you can be good enough.

ENTREPRENEUR INSIGHT:
Knowing Your Role

Sarah Ellis and Helen Tupper are co-founders of the career coaching company Amazing If and authors of The Squiggly Career. *As they see it, everyone has super strengths, and also areas in their skill set where they are not so hot. But as Sarah points out, weaknesses can be addressed.*

'We know our strengths. I am brilliant at spotting opportunities. Helen is brilliant at making things happen. Neither of us are good on detail,' she says. When you know your strengths, you know where you can make yourself most useful. You can concentrate on the things that make the most impact, and get out of your own way.

However, in weaker areas, you can be good enough. Sarah cites selling as a case in point. A self-acknowledged introvert, she admits that selling is not something she takes to naturally. 'But it is something that every entrepreneur should be able to do,' she adds. 'The way I do it is to develop trusted relationships.' I would agree – some people are naturally good at cold-calling or hard selling, but that has never been my strong suit. Where I succeed is in building a relationship or even a friendship with a client, and creating opportunities from there. At the end of the day, 'people buy from people', so trusted relationships are essential.

Someone once said that 'comparison is the thief of joy', and he was absolutely right. If you feel inferior to others, it will hold you back. If you think yourself superior, on the other hand, you may become complacent. Neither is helpful. So be aware of and aim to develop the skills and attributes you might be lacking, but avoid the comparison trap.

You're Never Too Old (or Young)

The comparison trap isn't always related to skills or experience. You might join an organization at a comparatively late stage in life, and find that most of your peers – particularly the movers and shakers – are ten years younger. The temptation is to create an ad hoc profile of what success looks like in that company, and conclude that you are too old.

If you are thinking about starting a business, you might make a similar assessment when you leaf through a trade magazine and find that it is profiling rising stars who are under thirty. So at forty or fifty, you think you're clearly over the hill.

Conversely, if you're only twenty, you might feel like you're too young to start a business, especially when you go along to a networking event and find it populated by people who benefit from the experience they've gained from years in the industry.

But the reality is that no one is too young or too old. What's important is the strengths that you bring to the table.

I remember vividly the experience of starting my first official business aged twenty-two, with all of the energy and enthusiasm – and some of the naivety – that comes with youth. One thing is for sure – I made mistakes. I also had many moments where I was extremely self-conscious about being the youngest person in the room. It took a lot of work on my personal brand and confidence to ensure that people began to see me for the work that I could do, the knowledge I did have, as opposed to the years of experience I didn't possess, at the time.

But my age also had its advantages – when I asked for help (which wasn't often), people were ready to rally around the brave young woman who had started a business and help where they could. The network I built was essential to the success I enjoy today.

One thing is for certain – and we have all experienced it – age does not always equate with wisdom.

Putting Your Head above the Parapet

Do anything that stands out from the crowd and you will attract attention, simply because you are putting your head above the parapet. This can be an uncomfortable experience. It puts you in the public eye. You'll be judged for what you do and, inevitably, not all of those judgements will be positive.

The first thing that has to be said is that you can't really control what people think of you. Indeed, in most cases, you won't even know. That doesn't mean you won't speculate and assume the worst, however. There's an unhelpful personality trait psychologists have dubbed 'mind-reading'. This is when you assume what another person is thinking. So, you might meet someone for the first time and think you are being negatively judged, even though there is no evidence.

It's important to avoid making assumptions about what other people think. Take pride in what you do, and let others think what they will.

But what about those times when people are upfront and brutal about what they think? Social media is a wonderful thing, and a brilliant marketing/branding tool, but it also encourages comments from keyboard warriors who can vent their spleen with little fear of comeback. For instance, you might post about something you're doing, or a new product you're selling, and back comes a barrage of personal abuse. There is no denying that this can be a source of anxiety, concern and even distress, even when the criticism is clearly unwarranted.

The only way around this is to accept that everyone has a right to an opinion and that not everyone will get you. Equally, you have a right to disagree with what they say. It's also worth remembering that the people who are quickest to criticize, condemn and belittle others are often revealing more about themselves than they like to think. If someone tells you that your business will never be a success (as an uncle of mine once did), that could be because they have harboured their own ultimately unfulfilled ambitions. The sight of someone else making an effort, putting in the hours and pursuing a big vision triggers regrets, insecurities and even resentment. This is then expressed through negative comments.

That's not to say you shouldn't pay attention to your reputation. It's important to think about your personal brand and how your business is perceived. Personal and business brand management are, in fact, the only ways you can have some control – or, to be more precise, influence – over the judgements that third parties will make.

So, do heed any warning signs. If just a few individuals are attacking you and/or your business, then fine – shrug it off. But if you are attracting a lot of bad online feedback, then it's probably time to look at your personal brand. What is it about your posts or online presence that triggers a negative response? Criticism is also feedback – and if used in the right way, feedback is always a gift.

Money (or the Lack of It)

Not all ventures require a huge amount of capital to get up and running. A bookkeeping business launched from a spare bedroom requires very little outlay. But others demand considerable upfront spending. Not surprisingly, then, one of the most commonly quoted reasons for not pursuing an entrepreneurial dream is simply this: 'I don't have enough money.'

Maybe at this point in time, you don't. But look around at your options, as there are a number of ways to solve the startup finance conundrum. In our previous book, *Self Made*, we covered six of the best sources of fast-track funding.

One of these is bootstrapping. Essentially, this is starting small, making sales, and financing the expansion of the business through the profits you make. For instance, if you're selling a product online, you might make or buy a small quantity to begin with. When all the units are sold, you can buy more. No major upfront investment is required.

Then there are the various flavours of crowdfunding. Rewards crowdfunding allows you to collect money in advance for a project. For example, you write a book and ask for contributions towards printing costs. Those who put up cash receive not only the book but also a reward, such as an invite to the launch. This technique effectively pre-funds your product by rewarding early adopters. You do, however, have to capture the collective imagination of potential funders.

Equity crowdfunding platforms enable you to sell shares in return for cash. This is a great way to raise cash while also bringing in a broad community of shareholders who can act as advocates. However, in most cases, investors will be looking for companies with significant growth potential.

Investment from friends and family should never be discounted. When I started my business I had just spent my life savings on buying a flat and didn't have all of the money needed for my venture, so I secured investments from friends who took shares in return. They still have those shares today.

You can even start a business on a credit card – using it to pay bills or buy stock. Byron's first business was launched with the help of a Capital One card, which provided enough money to attend training courses and set up an office. There are also bank loans, overdrafts, peer-to-peer lending platforms and – for more established businesses – solutions such as invoice finance, which allows you to borrow against the money owed to you by customers.

The bigger point here is that there are a great many sources of finance. If you believe in what you're doing, it should be possible to raise the capital you need.

But the 'I don't have enough money' issue can also arise when the time comes to take on staff for the first time, or increase the number of people on the company's payroll. You may see this as a cost. If you hire someone at £24,000 a year, that's £2,000 a month you have to find – plus other employer contributions. But that's not necessarily the right way to look at it. An employee will – or at least should – generate cash for the business. That might be because they are selling – and thus directly creating income – or because they are part of a team which ensures (through the magic of division of labour) that the venture runs more efficiently, produces more in the way of goods or services, and therefore makes a bigger profit.

It is more helpful to see new employees not in terms of what they will cost but rather what they will provide in terms of value. A new hire may take £2,000 a month in salary, but the same individual will potentially make a disproportionate contribution to an increase in revenues. That contribution is probably obvious if the new staff member is making sales, but the truth is that, regardless of function, we hire people to add value to the business – which can in turn increase sales, productivity and hopefully profit.

In that respect, the question should always be: will the new hire enhance the profitability of the business to a degree that justifies their salary? Maybe you don't know. If that's the case, you can always test the waters with a three-month probationary period.

The stresses of taking on employees stretch beyond the obvious financial concerns, however. You are putting faith in individuals who are essentially unknown quantities. People are unpredictable. They can look great on paper. They can promise you the world in their interview. And then when you offer them a job, maybe they don't show up (figuratively or even literally!).

So, how do you choose the right person? It's partly down to experience. As you interview more people, it will become easier to spot who is right for the role, as opposed to those who are simply saying all the right things. If you can afford to, recruit more people than you need. Then keep hold of the good ones.

From an employer's point of view, it's important to present a realistic picture of what the job entails. If you oversell – perhaps suggesting unattainable commissions or promising promotion opportunities that don't actually exist – you risk bringing people on board who will rapidly become disillusioned.

It's also worth asking candidates to call you back to tell you if they really want the job. This isn't normal practice, but it can be useful. At the end of the interview, you say: 'Go away and think for twenty-four hours. If you really want to do this, get back to me.' This effectively identifies those who want to work for you. The others will simply not ring back.

Once you've brought people on board, be clear when you're describing tasks, jobs and projects. Don't assume that people will know what you mean. Explaining everything carefully means staff will be less likely to make mistakes. They will be happier, and so will you.

The Perils of Procrastination

When we give ourselves reasons to put our plans on hold, one of two things tends to happen. Either we quietly give up, or we promise ourselves that, at some point in the future, our plans will get back on track. In other words, we procrastinate – constantly pushing what we really need to do into the near or distant future.

Procrastination can seem like a virtue. At school, I was a conscientious student. I read the assigned books, I went to the library and I did the work. But somewhere along the line, I told myself that I worked better under pressure. Although I would try to work steadily throughout the year, I would end up spending an awfully long time procrastinating. Pushing everything back resulted in me burning the candle at both ends when exams or deadlines were on the horizon. I always achieved under pressure and got it all done, so I told myself I worked best that way and that procrastination was a positive feature in my life.

But I am here to tell you now that, whatever you might think, a tendency to procrastinate is not a bonus. All it does is ensure that you are always stressed, constantly tired and quite possibly in a panic. Procrastination can be an easy habit to acquire and a hard one to break, but you can teach yourself some good habits.

Blocking out your time is a good place to start. Break your calendar or schedule down into manageable units of time. Once you've done that, create a plan by setting out your goals and the various things you need to do in order to reach your objectives. Those tasks can be slotted into the time blocks, giving you a clear route map.

ENTREPRENEUR INSIGHT:
Becoming 'Indistractable'

Nir Eyal is both an entrepreneur and an author. His book Indistractable *is a brilliantly practical guide to avoiding the procrastination that prevents us from achieving our goals. As he sees it, the ability to avoid distraction in a world where there are huge and diverse demands on our time is the 'skill of the century'.*

He cites the example of starting a perhaps simple but also arduous task – such as writing an article. 'Before writing, I used to have the same routine. I would say I'm going to begin the big piece. But first, let me check some email.'

And here's the trap. Because checking email feels like work too. What's more, it feels like urgent work. From dawn to dusk and beyond, your email is filling up with messages that may be important and also require a response. And for many of us, the same could be said for checking social media. So we become distracted.

'What's the opposite of distraction? Most people will say focus but that's not exactly true,' says Eyal. 'The opposite is traction. Traction moves you forward. Distraction stops you from becoming what you want to become.'

Eyal stresses that you don't need an iron will to avoid procrastination: 'People who perform well don't necessarily have superior willpower or self-control, but they do have a system.'

He also emphasizes the importance of scheduling. We may need to check our email or social media, but most of us do it too often – for two reasons. Firstly, it fills a gap. We feel lonely or insecure, so we try to find ways of creating the illusion of being more connected. Secondly, we prioritize the apparently urgent over the important.

Emails say to us: 'Answer me now.' This distracts us from the important matter of writing an article or preparing a client pitch.

To avoid distraction, Eyal recommends that we pre-decide how much time to spend on a range of activities (and when we'll do them) – whether that's watching Netflix, spending time with family, posting on social media or checking our email. Once we do that, we are back in control of our time.

It can be helpful to find a buddy or accountability partner – someone who can check in to see how much progress you're making on a task. Missing a deadline can be all too easy if you are accountable only to yourself. Knowing that someone will be calling to see how you're getting on is a spur to action. Ideally – if this is to work over the longer term – it should be a reciprocal arrangement that delivers a mutual benefit.

Don't forget your environment. It's important to find a space (or spaces) you feel comfortable working in. There isn't a right or wrong place. A student might like the university library because of the buzz of endeavour. A business owner starting a business at home might rent a desk in a shared workspace to be surrounded by a similar buzz. Whether it's a dedicated office, a back room at home, or a cafe, the space should be conducive to work. It's also a good idea to have snacks and water close to hand. After all, a walk to the fridge or the coffee machine is a well-known way to procrastinate.

It's important to strike a balance. Yes, create a plan, but don't beat yourself up if things fall behind a little. Because you have a schedule and you know where you need to be, you can always catch up. And neither should you beat yourself up looking for perfection. This can actually be another way of procrastinating – because nothing is ever quite perfect, so nothing ever gets finished.

EXERCISE:
Get It Done

Identify a goal or task, and a deadline for when you want to have accomplished it – something simple, like getting a website ready for the first day of the business.

Write down everything you need to do to achieve your goal. In the website example, this might include:

- Deciding on the pages needed for the launch – home page, About page, product guide, contacts page, etc.
- Sketching out the content for each page – what information do you need to convey?
- Deciding who will write the content – will you do it or hire someone?
- Writing the content, or finding the person you're going to hire and briefing them.
- Hiring a designer and agreeing a process.
- Buying a domain name.

Once you have all the steps written down, work out a rough sequence and timeline. Divide your schedule or calendar into blocks of time, and assign one or more of the necessary tasks to each block.

Using Social Media Effectively

Social media is arguably procrastination's closest friend. There was a time when a founder working alone in an office had only a limited menu of distractions to choose from. A walk to the fridge, a sudden desire to rearrange the furniture, or perhaps just calling up a friend to talk about not very much.

Today, social media puts distraction in front of all of our noses.

It's a distraction on steroids. Facebook, Instagram, YouTube, Tik-Tok, Pinterest – they're all ready and waiting to soak up our precious time. And, of course, that is exactly what they were designed to do. Social media creates a fear of missing out, so we're constantly checking newsfeeds to see what friends and competitors are up to. And when we ourselves post, the hit of dopamine that courses through our bodies when it's liked, shared or commented upon ensures that we constantly come back. That's the idea, anyway.

That's not to say that social media is a bad thing. On a personal level, the various platforms offer a great way to stay in touch with friends. And if you're running a business, it's probably the most cost-effective channel through which to raise your profile and create a brand.

Byron and I aim to be omnipresent, and that includes having a presence on social media – to put ourselves 'out there'. But we're aware that it's something that should be approached intelligently. And that applies to how you present yourself – as adding value to a community is generally much better than simply promoting a product – and to the amount of time you spend online.

Put simply, social media shouldn't dominate your working life. As you grow your business, you'll find there are a great many tedious tasks that are essential. It's all too easy to let the temptation of checking Instagram or watching a video on YouTube blow you off course. And once you've started following a thread or got to the end of a video, one thing can lead to another. Before you know it, you've wasted half an hour or longer.

So, try to limit your time on social media, and – as we've mentioned before – don't get hung up on other people's comments.

A Winning Mindset

Obstacles – both external and those you have placed in your own way – are there to be overcome. And, make no mistake, you will encounter your share of hurdles. To get past them, you need to adopt a winning mindset.

A winning mindset can be characterized quite simply. Winners deal with whatever is in front of them. Losers give up.

Let's look at an example. The Covid-19 crisis is still fresh in all our memories, and for business owners it generated some potentially business-ending challenges. That was particularly true for companies that rely on face-to-face interaction in physical spaces, as during the lockdown, social contact was largely suspended. As we all know, cafes, bars, restaurants, hotels, gyms and other hospitality and leisure companies saw their customers and revenues disappear. Training businesses also suffered, which was something that I experienced personally. As the implications of the lockdown became apparent, one of my clients cancelled a series of bookings worth £22,000.

My response to this setback was crucial. Someone with a losing mindset might, at that point, have said: 'That's it. It's all over. It's done. I can't survive this.' But the winning mindset looks for solutions, and assesses both the long- and the short-term implications.

In this case, one option would have been to insist on payment. It was a late cancellation, and I could have asked for the sum in full. Yet that wouldn't have been the right thing to do. Yes, receiving £22,000 would undoubtedly have felt like a satisfying short-term win in a difficult time. But – and this is a very big but – I could have lost the client for ever.

The better answer was to find a middle ground, and so I suggested moving the session online. A one-off virtual event was less valuable in the short term than the bigger booking, but it enabled me to continue building a relationship with the client while also exploring new ways of working. I was supporting them through a difficult period, and people always remember those who pivot and are helpful in a time of need.

All the way through the pandemic, we saw examples of businesses who changed their way of working in order to keep afloat and position themselves for a better future. Restaurants transformed into takeaway and delivery services. Travel firms used the gap in bookings to forge industry partnerships. Retailers stepped up online sales. This was the winning mindset writ large across the economy.

And as entrepreneur Paul Jarvis points out, smaller businesses proved particularly flexible: 'Small businesses have an advantage because they can adapt very quickly. We've seen that during the pandemic, how small businesses were able to move fast. They have autonomy.' Alternatively you may be a smaller department in a large organization. If you have the liberty to leverage your size, then use it to your advantage.

Developing Your Mindset

Everyone is different. Some people naturally have (or adopt) a winning mindset as their default position. But if that's not you, here's the good news: a winning mindset can be developed.

Observing the habits of successful people is a good place to start. How do they conduct themselves? How do they deal with the setbacks, tensions and trigger points that are an intrinsic part of doing business? What can you learn from them?

Unless you're lucky enough to live next door to Elon Musk or Folorunso Alakija, that might seem a tall order. But there are plenty of ways to learn what successful people are really like. Biographies, profile interviews in newspapers and magazines, videos on YouTube – all of these sources will give you insights into their mindset.

That's not to say, however, that you should constantly be observing the already rich and famous in search of tips. The habit of a winning mindset can equally be developed within a successful circle of peers. For instance, you may have friends who are already running businesses. Spend time with them. Learn from them, and compare notes. And if you don't have such a group among the people you already know, cultivate or join a circle of winners via networking events or mentoring communities.

The other side of this particular coin is that it's not a great idea to spend a lot of time in a circle where the general mindset is negative. If members of your peer group are shocked and concerned when you announce a plan to quit work and launch a business, their scepticism is likely to seep into your self-perception. In this case, it's time to find a new circle. We're not saying you should dump all your old friends. But you should aim to spend more time with people who will support you.

Which brings us to one often overlooked aspect of the winning mindset: winners like to see other people win. We have found that in our mentoring community, one of the real bonuses for our mentees is the support system they provide for each other. The support they have received both from us as mentors and from their fellow mentees has helped them to thrive, and they delight in the success of others and make a point of lifting up those around them. This is an attitude you should develop.

Be Grateful

Success is not something that happens in isolation. There will be people who provide help and support when you're just getting started. There will be members of your team who go above and beyond the call of duty. You will gain loyal and regular customers. This is worth remembering. You will have reason to be grateful to a lot of people.

And it's actually a pretty good idea to express that gratitude. Pick your time – Christmas or a birthday, maybe – and let your stakeholders know that their support is genuinely appreciated. You can send them a card, drop them an email or give them a call. It's the sentiment that matters.

Perhaps a bigger point to make here is that an open and optimistic approach to life often correlates quite neatly with a winning mindset. It's very easy to get wrapped up in your own projects, perhaps to the exclusion of everything else. But actually it makes sense, both personally and professionally, to be curious about and interested in what other people – and not necessarily just those in your industry or peer group – are doing and saying. People are always willing to give advice. And while you'll hear a lot of rubbish – people talk a lot of rubbish – you'll occasionally come across a nugget of truth. Something that's very useful.

I say all this to highlight that tensions will always arise in business – but most of the time they arise from problems that you can solve. So be positive and proactive. No excuses. No blaming others, no complaining and no wasting time. You are in business to win. As author and businessman Grant Cardone put it: 'In life, you don't get what you desire, you get what you work your ass off for.'

So get your sh*t together, and make it work.

Chapter Four

Cope When Things Go Wrong

*'Life is full of enough misfortunes without
increasing them by inventing others.'*

– Michel de Montaigne

Very few people can claim to have genuinely helped millions of people around the world to achieve success and fully realize their potential.

Brian Tracy is one of the select few. The bestselling author of more than eighty books and an in-demand public speaker, his focus is the psychology of achievement. Whether your goal is to become better at selling, to maximize your potential as an effective business leader or to achieve certain ambitious personal goals, Brian's books and speaking engagements are a great way of immersing yourself in practical advice and inspiration.

So, when Bianca and I decided to promote an event with Brian as the main speaker, we couldn't have been more excited. Here was a chance to meet and work with someone who we greatly admired, while also putting together a programme that would inspire and motivate all who attended. In all honesty, staging the event was a very big deal.

Naturally, we worked extremely hard to ensure it all went well. We invested thousands of pounds in marketing and hiring a venue. And the hard work paid off. All the tickets sold, and when we looked at the bookings we were surprised to see that people were coming not only from the UK but from around the world. All was set for a great day.

And then?

Well, in business things go wrong – and sometimes things go

very, very, very wrong. In this case, Brian's agent rang us at short notice to tell us that, due to health reasons, he wouldn't be able to attend.

So, we had a venue booked, tickets sold and a huge amount of expectation. We also had a very large blank space in the programme. We had to find a solution.

Welcome to the world of the entrepreneur. No matter how well and thoroughly you plan, there will always be setbacks, and very often they turn up out of a clear, blue sky, with very little warning. Sometimes, they are relatively minor – and can be dealt with quickly – but every so often you are faced with a situation that seems, initially at least, to be sitting on a spectrum that runs from difficult to absolutely impossible.

What matters is how you respond.

In the heat of the moment – when a piece of bad news first drops – you may be gripped by some difficult and uncomfortable emotions. Fear, perhaps – or its close relation, panic. As the implications of the bad news begin to sink in, your stress and anxiety levels are likely to rise. And over the longer term, that anxiety may become entrenched. In the case of long-term problems, this can evolve into depression.

Emotions and reactions such as fear, stress and even to some degree anxiety are not necessarily negative. They are your brain's way of telling you that something bad or difficult is happening, and that it needs to be dealt with. The other side of the coin, however, is that the same feelings can drag you down. As an entrepreneur, you are going to have to build resilience and develop strategies that will enable you to deal with tough situations and the emotions that arise from them.

That's what we'll be looking at in this chapter.

Negative Impact

So what are we dealing with here? Well, you can think of fear, panic, stress and anxiety as a kind of family of responses to situations and circumstances that have the potential to undermine your business or indeed your overall sense of wellbeing

But these are not interchangeable words. As defined by the American Psychiatric Association, 'fear' is a response to a specific situation or set of circumstances that is genuinely (or perceived to be) threatening. It's an immediate thing and it often passes very quickly, either because you run from the danger (flight) or face it down (fight). It can also be a response to a perceived future situation or set of circumstances, as in the case of a fear of failure or a fear of what is on the other side of success.

So, if you're standing on a pavement and you see a car spinning out of control in your direction, you will probably – and quite rightly – feel fear. In an ideal world, fear will trigger the fight-or-flight response that is embedded in your brain to get you out of danger. In the case of a car rushing in your direction, flight – or at least jumping out of the way – is the wisest course of action.

Panic, on the other hand, is considered to be a much less focused emotion. You could characterize it as an uncontrolled response to a threat. Generally speaking, panic is not a good thing, not least because it can lead to unpredictable and counterproductive behaviour that actually increases the risk of harm. Going back to our speeding car, a panicked reaction may see you frozen to the spot.

Then there are panic attacks. These are usually related to some deep-seated source of concern. Often with very little warning, an individual can be seized by a sense that something bad is about to happen. Then physical symptoms set in – sometimes dizziness and quick, uncontrolled breathing. It can feel like you're having a heart attack, thus escalating the panic. People often feel a sense of panic when they start worrying, whether consciously or unconsciously, about what might happen in the future.

Stress is something different again. Rather like fear, stress tends to be linked to something that is clearly identifiable, but in this case it's something that exerts pressure over a period of time. It may happen on one of those afternoons when you're rushing – and battling against the odds – to meet a delivery deadline. Or it may happen over weeks, months or even years. For example, if a business is struggling to regularly generate enough cash to pay its employees and suppliers, that is likely to be a major source of stress over the long term.

Medium- and long-term stress can result in sleeplessness, constant worrying and irritability. It can also trigger physical symptoms, such as fatigue and a faster heart rate. If not dealt with, long-term health problems can develop.

And over time, stress can become something more deep-seated – namely anxiety. Over the short term, anxiety is a response to stressful or worrying circumstances, and the symptoms of stress – a lack of sleep, worrying, mood changes, etc. – apply. But severe anxiety, diagnosed as generalized anxiety disorder (GAD), is not only considered a mental health condition in its own right, it is also associated with depressive episodes, potentially leading to a seemingly constant low mood and feelings of powerlessness.

A sense of fear, a panic response, and short-term stress or long-term anxiety – these are all responses that can be triggered by specific events or circumstances. In some cases, you may need to seek help from a medical professional, but there are also strategies that can help you overcome rising negative emotions.

A Catalyst for Action

As an entrepreneur, it is vitally important to see negative triggers for what they are and subsequently manage the situation towards a positive outcome.

Fear of a bad outcome can be the catalyst that triggers an effective response, provided you can channel your concern into actions that make a difference. Fear – in a business context – is your brain telling you in no uncertain terms that the outcome of an event will have real and damaging consequences. For instance, you might hear through the grapevine that your biggest client has been looking for an alternative supplier and may cancel a lucrative contract within weeks. The fear of a major blow to your company prompts an urgent 'fight' reaction that results in you doing everything you can to retain the business.

This is not to be confused with panic – which may also set in momentarily, but shouldn't be allowed to take hold. A panicked reaction might see you sending an ill-thought-out email to your client within minutes of hearing the news. An email that perhaps gives away too much about your own insecurities and the source of your information. You don't really know what to say, but you say it anyway. The email could do more harm than good.

Stress – at its most positive – can also be extremely useful. There are people who thrive on a certain amount of stress, as it provides the adrenalin rush that gets them through the working day. Rather like fear, stress can be seen as an acknowledgement that the task you're engaged in matters. It has to be executed well and delivered on time. The thing about positive stress, however, is that it ultimately relies on a sense that, no matter how hard the day gets, you – along with the members of your team – are in the driving seat.

Workplace stress begins to take on a more difficult hue when that sense of control is lost. When the impossible task really is impossible. Or when the level of work required to fulfil a mission is not a temporary spike but something that is constant and unrelenting.

What we all need to develop within ourselves is the means to respond to difficult circumstances in a way that acknowledges the scale or seriousness of the problem, while also equipping us to successfully resolve the situation.

Sources of Fear

Perhaps 'fear' seems too strong a word to you. After all, most business owners seldom encounter situations that involve any kind of physical threat. But fear doesn't have to take the form of a charging bull or a cobra ready to strike. There are plenty of situations that – although less primal – can cause fear or a creeping sense of panic.

For example, you might have a fear of not living up to expectations – either your own or those of others. Let's say you've quit your job and started a business. Your own expectation is that you will make a good living while being in control of your destiny. And you've probably told a few people about your big, audacious plans. At least some aspect of your sense of self rests upon making the venture a success.

So naturally, there is fear here too. Fear that you might fail. That all the things you've set out to achieve won't actually come to pass. That you'll let yourself down, and in a very public way. Maybe this fear was at its strongest the day you quit your old job. And maybe it re-emerges after the first week of trading, when the optimism of the business plan isn't reflected in early sales figures.

That fear of not living up to expectations could equally apply to the situation Bianca and I found ourselves in when we set up the event featuring Brian Tracy. Cancelling the event would have felt like a very public failure, which was yet another reason to find a solution.

Closely related to this is fear of the unknown. Quitting your job to start a business means – for most people – stepping out of your comfort zone and into territory that is very, very unfamiliar. Once, you earned a wage. Now you are the person responsible for generating the revenues that will pay you, your staff, your suppliers and possibly a commercial landlord. As an employee, you simply turn up every day, do your job to the best of your ability, and you don't have to worry about how much cash is flowing in and out of the business. Now everything is down to you. Until you're up and running and the business is on an upward trajectory, you don't know if you're going to be successful. It's a big unknown.

Fast-forward a decade and the fear could be of losing everything. The business has been going well for a while. Then one major client goes bust and another chooses an alternative supplier. Suddenly and unexpectedly, it's become much harder to make payroll, pay rent and honour the loan taken out to buy new equipment.

There will likely be smaller fears too. An invitation to address a major industry conference brings to the surface a hitherto-unnoticed terror of public speaking. Or you may have a fear of networking – especially when it involves walking into a room of complete strangers and starting conversations. These are not necessarily direct threats to your business (unless public speaking is part of your revenue model), but a failure to overcome them could prevent you from doing something useful, rewarding or lucrative.

Fear triggers your fight or flight. If you opt for flight, you get out of the way of the problem. But a fight response enables you to overcome the hurdle that stands in your way, and that can only be a good thing.

And you may well surprise yourself. In dealing with your fear, you might find that public speaking isn't quite so bad after all. Maybe doing it was actually a lot of fun. Because once you've done what you set out to do – whether that's starting a business or giving a presentation or organizing an event featuring a star speaker – you've taken your achievement to a whole new level. You've conquered your fear.

Sources of Stress

But business isn't always a succession of easy-to-jump hurdles. Sometimes difficult situations stretch out over a period of time and become a source of stress or anxiety.

We've talked about the positive side of stress – the response we have when a situation arises that needs to be dealt with under time pressure. Failure to meet a client deadline isn't an option, so everyone has to work above capacity for a limited period of time. It's tough, sometimes tempers fray, but when it's over, everyone feels good. There's a sense of achievement.

But what if every day is like that? What if, for whatever reason, you and your team are under unrelenting pressure to fulfil orders, and it begins to show? There might be resignations and a drop in morale. Maybe the business isn't making enough money to hire more people and cash flow becomes a problem. Anxiety sets in. It's time to do something about it.

Counter-intuitively, success can also generate stress. Think of the ambitious and bold startup that begins to grow rapidly. When there are just five or six people in the office, everything is fine. The founder hand-picks the staff and the culture is great. Then the scale-up operation begins. More staff are hired, which in turn results in an increasing number of conflicts that have to be resolved. Not everyone is pulling their weight, and those who are working hard are beginning to resent those who appear to be coasting. There is staff conflict and also a problem with leadership – i.e. how do you deal with the perfectly nice person in accounts who is consistently behind on sending out invoices? Meanwhile, expansion has meant taking on bigger but more demanding clients. Some of them have negotiated longer payment terms, which in turn means that managing cash flow has become an onerous task. Things are going well, but stress levels and possibly also anxiety levels have risen.

Or perhaps there's something specific about your business that niggles at you. Something that just doesn't sit right. For instance, one of my businesses is in the property services sector. For a long time, we were sending people in to carry out plumbing maintenance. It made money, but it also involved gas and the liabilities were huge if something went wrong. For me, it was a source of real concern. I worried about this aspect of the operation constantly. In the end, I solved the problem by agreeing to hand over the running of that side of the operation to my business partner, who was less risk-adverse and was happy to manage it. Always ask yourself, 'Am I the best person for this role, or would someone else be better placed to fill it?'

ENTREPRENEUR INSIGHT:
Mental Health in Business

'The quality of our mental health determines how we function, so it literally impacts absolutely everything. Not just work, but life – personal, professional, everything,' says James Routledge, founder of mental health support organization Sanctus.

As an entrepreneur, James struggled with his own mental health issues. Realizing that he wasn't enjoying his job, he reached out to others in the founders community for advice and support. This experience led to the creation of Sanctus, which offers coaching to employees and business owners and provides them with a space to talk about mental health issues.

And as James sees it, finding that 'space to talk' is vital. 'The difficulty with mental health is that to talk about it in any form, we have to show some vulnerability and perhaps expose our more messy or insecure parts,' he says. 'We have to say "I need help" or "I'm not sure", and that can be hard. We all have to find more safe spaces, to feel able to be vulnerable and share openly.'

Other people can certainly help. James suggests talking to 'confidants, peers who get it, partners, co-founders, communities and people/places where you feel like you can just say it how it is' and cites his own experience as CEO of Sanctus. Just as reaching out to others in the community had resulted in the creation of the company, it also helped James when he found himself struggling with his role: 'I wrote to a founders community I'm in and I said, "I'm not enjoying my job" – opening up like that to a group of people I can trust was a huge step for me.' It also led to James appointing a CEO and focusing on other aspects of the business.

That was a reaction to an ongoing situation, but James also stresses the importance of being proactive in prioritizing your mental health, without being overly prescriptive. 'If I tell people to do ten things before 6 a.m. for their mental health, it's just another thing to feel sh*t about. It's got to be a personal commitment to wanting to feel good, calm and relaxed, and not a ball of stress and anxiety constantly.'

So what does that mean in practice? 'Writing stuff down is a great place to start. Ask yourself, "What is causing me stress and anxiety?" Then just write. You can write every morning, just what's on your mind. Journaling is a great reflective practice.'

But what then? 'Everyone is different and I believe we all have to take our own steps to find out what works for us. What do we need to heal? What is holding us back? What supports us? What soothes us? We can only answer these questions as individuals. Mindfulness practices like meditation and journaling are a good start, and then spaces like coaching and therapy can support us in answering some of these questions and developing more self-knowledge and resilience,' he says.

It's also important to set boundaries. 'Saying no is a big part of boundaries, and in my experience saying no is good for mental health and good for business too,' says James. Equally, staying focused on your own purpose and reason for living plays a crucial role in maintaining a healthy mind. 'Find what gives you energy and do more of that – do what nourishes you and feeds your soul. That's when you'll be at your best.'

Be a Warrior, Not a Worrier

Here's the thing – the way to deal with fear or rising levels of stress is to find a solution. The solution may be simple, or it may take a while. But nine times out of ten there will be a way of resolving even the most difficult situation. A considered plan is the enemy of the worry, fear and anxiety that can hold you back from achieving your goals.

One way to think of it is this. Human beings are hardwired to look for problems and threats. This is what has helped us to survive. Sometimes we perceive threats that are not really there. For instance, late at night you might see something moving in the bushes and your fight-or-flight reaction kicks in. In reality, it's just a shadow created by a street light. But this is actually a good thing. It is better – in terms of survival – to react to false threats or 'false positives' than to ignore every hint of danger and believe it will all be fine.

When we're reacting to threats, whether real or perceived, we're using the part of our brain that developed in the first humans. In psychological terms, the savannah was an 'immediate return environment'. In other words, you had to react instantly to events to avoid facing death or injury

Today, we live in a 'delayed return environment'. The outcomes of our actions may not become apparent for months or even years. Start a business in January and you might not make real progress until the autumn. But because we're built to respond to danger, we worry. We see threats in situations where there is no actual danger, which is linked to that evolutionary tendency to expect the worst. Indeed, we often focus on negative events.

We see this in our lives every day. Think of the average evening news bulletin. It's mostly – although not always – focused on events that are concerning, unsettling or threatening: wars, famine, national divisions over Brexit, falling stock markets, environmental degradation. And as the Covid-19 pandemic illustrated, the more immediately threatening the situation, the more we turn to the news and also social media to find out more. There is good news all around us, of course – and some of it is reported – but it's usually the bad news that excites the greatest interest. And this can feed into a perception that the world is a more hazardous place than it actually is.

Often, we overstate the problem. According to research carried out at the Pennsylvania State University by Michelle Newman and Lucas LaFreniere, 91.4 per cent of the things we worry about actually never come to pass. But even if the worry *is* justified, it's important not to let it overwhelm or undermine you. One of the keys to success in business is to become a warrior, not a worrier. The former deals with situations decisively. The latter – well, the latter worries to no great effect.

Yvette Noel-Schure (better known as Beyoncé's publicist) provided a neat illustration of what that means in practice when we interviewed her for this book. A few minutes into our Zoom session, a call came in from a famous musician – one of her clients, who had a problem that needed to be fixed rapidly. Within a few minutes, a difficult situation had been resolved.

'I always try to stay calm,' she told us. 'And I try to make sure I fix everything within four or five minutes. And if I can't fix it, I find someone who can.'

The Warrior's Options

Which brings us neatly back to Brian Tracy. This was an example of a genuine problem. Cancellation of the event would have involved a certain amount of work – perhaps a considerable amount, in fact – to manage the reputational damage. If we cancelled this show – having sold so many tickets – would we be able to put together something similar in the future? Our credibility was at stake.

After the initial fear – in this case, fear of not living up to expectations – it would have perhaps been easy to descend into a long, drawn-out period of stress and anxiety. Instead, we began to look at the available options. From one point of view, the most obvious course of action was still cancellation – you could see this as 'flight'. Set aside the wounded pride and audience disappointment for a moment, and the case for simply calling the whole thing off could be made to sound compelling. We could contact everyone who had planned to attend, explain the situation and offer a refund. Handled well, maybe the reputational damage wouldn't be too bad.

There was another solution, however. We could find a replacement speaker and carry on. But the question we now faced was this: how would our audience feel?

Finding the answer to that question required us to focus on the problem through a very specific lens. What was the purpose of this event, and why were people attending? Were they, for example, solely going because of Brian, or had they signed up because of the event programme as a whole and the themes that Bianca and I had put together?

With the clock ticking, we did some research. What we found was that people wanted to attend anyway. Brian was a major attraction, but the programme as a whole was strong. Our own reputation – as entrepreneurs and speakers – was also seen as an important draw.

In other words, we could do it. We could carry on.

So we found an alternative keynote speaker – happily, in the shape of Brian's son. And on the day, he gave a great and inspiring presentation. An event that could have been a disaster turned out to be a triumph.

A Fight Strategy

Admittedly, getting there wasn't easy. Like everyone else in a similar position, we ran the gamut of emotions. And there were physical symptoms too – nausea, anxiety, an inability to sleep, some grey hairs (according to Bianca) and a sense of the room spinning.

In the short term, there are things you can do to help push back these reactions. For instance, you might:

- Take a deep breath
- Go for a walk to clear your head
- Do something to relax, like listen to music
- Go to a favourite restaurant, bar or club (in my case, that would be my private members' club)
- Turn off your devices (escaping the cascade of emails or social media messages can help you find the space to think)
- Meditate or pray

These are all things you can do to help free up the mental band-width you'll need to address the problem, but they don't solve the problem. In fact, if the problem is urgent, spending too long chilling in the woods or relaxing at your favourite bar might mean the situation slips away from you.

So your first task is to assess the urgency of what is unfolding. Have you got time to reflect? What would happen if you were to take twenty-four hours out? Would that give you valuable thinking time? Or would it simply waste time?

Let's assume here that you're facing an urgent problem – one that has to be resolved quickly. You've looked at your fight-or-flight options and you've made a decision to fight. Now you need a fight plan.

Essentially, there are three sequential steps, which can be applied to just about any situation. They are:

1. Assessment
2. Planning
3. Execution

Assessment

A clear-headed assessment of the situation is key to a successful resolution. No two situations are the same – not least in terms of seriousness. Some of the setbacks you encounter may appear major at the time but will actually be relatively simple to solve or less impactful than you first think. Conversely, some situations – once you begin to think them through – could be much more serious than you originally thought.

In other words, you need to assess the impact.

Then you need to think about a timeline. This won't always be straightforward. In the case of our Brian Tracy conference, we had a clear deadline based on the fact that people would be arriving for the event. Thus, we had to formulate a plan very, very quickly.

In other cases, timing is important but not necessarily something you can pin down to a specific day or even month. For instance, you might have a nagging worry about the exposure of your business to just two, three or four big customers. One customer going elsewhere could be a disaster, and so you need to build in resilience by taking on more clients. But how soon do you need to act?

You can try a thought experiment when you're facing a situation that requires action. Ask yourself: 'What happens if I don't do anything today? What impact will that have?' If there won't be much impact, you probably have a little more time to assess the problem and make plans.

And that in turn will mean there is time to seek help in assessing the situation. If you have a mentor – or mentors – speak to them. Get a new perspective on the problem. Remember, you're in the thick of things, and that isn't always the best place to be when you need to think clearly. A mentor will help you to step back and take a more objective view.

Planning and Execution

Assessing the situation enables you to take control. The next step is to plan exactly what you're going to do. Based on your overall view of the impact and seriousness of the problem, you need to find a way through to the other side.

Let's go back to the event Bianca and I had organized. Once we decided to press ahead, we needed to do everything possible to ensure that we could do so successfully. So, we had to consider an alternative speaker and arrange the booking. Bringing Brian Tracy's son on board was an important part of the plan. In addition, we had to think about how to rearrange the programme and keep attendees informed.

If the source of your stress is low sales, or you're worried about relying on a few customers, you will need to put a comprehensive plan together to turn the situation around. This could take time and energy. In fact, we could be talking about a full-scale business recalibration, with goals, milestones and action points. Taking on more customers could involve increasing capacity – and that could, in turn, require more staff. So, essentially, you're setting new goals and coming up with new timelines (see Chapter Two).

If stress due to overwork is the problem, the plan might well involve changing how you work. Perhaps you've realized that instead of doing everything yourself, you need to delegate. So how will that work? Do you need to bring people in, or hand over more responsibility to an existing employee? What training will be required?

And finally, you'll need to put the whole plan into action. You stage the event. You find more customers. You delegate to a manager.

Contingency Plans and Shock Absorbers

So far we've assumed that the sources of your (hopefully temporary) fear, panic, stress and anxiety have happened unexpectedly. They're an unpleasant surprise and you have to deal with them. And it's certainly true that anyone in business will usually be on the receiving end of any number of shocks. You don't know when your speaker will cancel. You don't know that a pandemic is going to hit. You won't necessarily be aware that your best salesperson is about to join a competitor. But what you can do in preparation is to game out possible scenarios and assess the impact on your business – and, if necessary, make contingency plans.

Think of it this way. You're about to drive from London to Scotland. It's a long way and the road can be bumpy. But that's OK, because your car – like all cars – has built-in shock absorbers. In business, your contingency plans are your shock absorbers.

Whatever venture you undertake, there will be things that can go wrong and some of them will be very obvious. For example, if you happen to be organizing a public event, it will probably cross your mind that one or more of the speakers might cancel. The chances are this won't happen, but it might. It's an identifiable risk.

Once you've recognized that possibility, you can begin to think about what that would mean in terms of negative impact. We've talked about the reputational damage that might be caused by cancelling an event. But there is probably a financial price to pay too. Tickets have to be refunded, and the venue will still want to be paid. Then there is all the money thrown into marketing. So one type of contingency plan is insurance. If an event is cancelled (in line with the reasons specified on the policy), the insurer will pay out.

Insurance brings with it a certain peace of mind. When Bianca and I booked Brian Tracy, we were insured – and that fact definitely provided a degree of comfort. But the insurance doesn't always cover everything that went into the planning and creation of the event.

Contingency planning can take a lot of different forms. If fire or flood strikes your office, you could well lose all your paperwork, including your customer data and invoices. Unless, of course, you've backed everything up securely elsewhere. Another aspect of your planning for such a scenario might be a home office where you and your colleagues can work until your normal building is open and usable again.

Then there is financial planning. For instance, when a business owner takes out a bank loan, the lender will usually want to see a business plan that includes best- and worst-case scenarios. The loan may be comfortably repayable as things stand, but what if revenues drop 10 or 20 per cent for a period? Is there is a risk of defaulting on the loan? The bank will want to see evidence of contingency planning so they know the business can handle the impact of a sudden and unexpected downturn.

It's also worth planning for a degree of staff churn. What if one of your sales team is responsible for more than 50 per cent of orders, despite representing just one-eighth of the department's personnel? And what if they leave the company? This is actually very likely, given that good salespeople are in high demand. Contingency planning might include a three-month notice period (to allow time to recruit a replacement), or implementing a training and development programme now to bring the rest of the team up to speed.

All of these scenarios are things that can be planned for if you spend a bit of time looking for weak spots in the business – such as over-reliance on a star player – or external factors that could have a serious impact. If any of these factors poses a genuine threat to your ability to trade and thrive, you should be making a contingency plan to deal with it.

EXERCISE:
Contingency Planning

- Sit down with some sheets of paper.
- List some potential threats to your business – one per page.
- Assess the impact of each threat (e.g. emerging competitors, changing regulatory environment, negative press/media coverage, changing attitudes).
- Write down a contingency plan for each.

The pandemic of 2020 tested the ability of a great many businesses to not only deal with stress but also find a way through to the other side. Entrepreneur Paul Jarvis offers three tips on how to do this. 'When crises like the 2020 sh*tshow arise, you need to be resilient, you need to accept the reality as it is and you need to be able to be adaptable – to roll with the punches,' he says.

As he sees it, that ties in with having a sense of purpose – 'a North Star that reminds you what you're working towards'. Paul cites the example of a huge internet outage which massively affected his own internet privacy business, Fathom. 'It wasn't our fault, but we had to do something about it. We know that internet privacy is a hugely important issue for our clients. So we were constantly in touch with them. Keeping them updated. It was our sense of purpose that spurred us to do that.'

The Business Rollercoaster

It's a little bit like passing your driving test. You can drive on your own, but over the next few weeks and months you'll have experiences on the road that you didn't encounter in the instructor's car. And every new experience is a chance to learn. Each journey will teach you something new, but don't expect things to get easier straight away.

To use another analogy, it's like getting on a big rollercoaster for the first time. The car climbs, drops and that's fine, but when it loops the loop, you find yourself desperately hanging on to your wallet to stop it sliding out of your pocket, and your sunglasses fall off.

Then the ride ends and it was a buzz. You want to get on again, so this time you get yourself organized. New sunglasses are buttoned into your pocket, as is your wallet. But this time, you find yourself dribbling – not a good look.

But you get on again, and again, and then you go to places where there are bigger rollercoasters. Each time the experience gets better, but it is never the same. There are always new things to learn.

Chapter Five

Overcome Imposter Syndrome and Self-Limiting Beliefs

'There are still days I wake up feeling like a fraud,
not sure I should be where I am.'

– Sheryl Sandberg

Everything has gone more or less exactly to plan. You have a flourishing entrepreneurial career, the respect of your peers, and an impressive list of personal and professional achievements on your CV. And yet sometimes you wake up in the morning and none of this seems quite real. Yes, things have gone well, but maybe that's down to luck rather than drive, determination, knowledge and business acumen on your part. At times, your inner voice tells you that, despite all the success, you're a bit of a fraud.

If you recognize that feeling, then it may well be that you're suffering from imposter syndrome. Put simply, it's a mindset – or psychological pattern – that causes you to question and doubt your own accomplishments. Instead of feeling good about what you've achieved to date, you dwell – even if only occasionally – on the possibility that your success has been largely accidental and that you shouldn't really be where you are today. And more worryingly, despite all evidence to the contrary, you are dogged by the perception (or more accurately, the self-perception) that you don't really know what you're doing. As these feelings grow, so does the fear that other people will eventually see through you. That you will be found out.

Fear of being exposed as an imposter can dog even the most successful individuals. Michelle Obama has been an inspiration to millions of women around the world and yet, speaking to an audience of students at the Elizabeth Garrett Anderson School in London, she acknowledged that she too is sometimes gripped by self-doubt, telling them: 'I still have a little [bit of] imposter syndrome – it never goes away.'

ENTREPRENEUR INSIGHT:
Period of Imposter Syndrome

Sarah Ellis and Helen Tupper founded their coaching company, Amazing If, after enjoying successful careers in the corporate world. 'Imposter syndrome probably stopped us starting our business earlier,' says Sarah. 'We were very anchored to the success we'd had in the organizations that we'd worked in, and that felt so far away from running your own business. You always think that it's practical things that are going to stop you running a business, but for me it was emotional. I had to ask myself, could I let go of working for a big business and all the things like an impressive job title? And then I thought, "What if that's what I'm good at – working in a big corporation?"'

'I think it did stop us,' agrees Helen. 'I didn't come from an entrepreneurial background. My parents were both career-ladder people, so entrepreneurship wasn't my context. I think what gave me confidence was knowing that I had saleable strengths. If the business folded, then I could use those strengths to get another job.'

It's important to note that imposter syndrome isn't merely a retrospective cloud of negative self-perception that crosses the otherwise-blue skies of the world's most successful people. It can emerge (and re-emerge) at just about any point in life or a business journey.

It could be there on day one of your first business. You throw open the doors of that cafe you've always dreamed of running and the thought suddenly strikes you: 'Should I really be doing this? What do I know about catering?' Or you turn up for your first meeting at the offices of a prospective customer. You face a panel of buyers, all of whom know their industry inside out, and something inside you says: 'I really don't belong here.' Further down the line, you might be asked to do an interview about your business for local radio or a newspaper. But your internal voice is saying: 'I don't deserve this.'

I found myself dealing with a form of imposter syndrome ahead of my first major public-speaking engagement. I started asking myself if I really had a right to be there. Would the people in the audience take me seriously? Was I the sort of person that could inspire others to follow my path, to start a business? It wasn't a comfortable feeling.

Imposter syndrome can affect our personal lives too, not just our business performance. In relationships, it's not uncommon for one partner to feel that the other is 'out of their league'. This can lead to the relationship needlessly ending, because the insecurities of one person throw the whole thing off balance. Ironically, however, the imposter effect can form the basis of a highly successful relationship – simply because the insecure partner doesn't give up on trying to please the other.

Something You Can Deal With (But Not Conquer)

For the most part, though, imposter syndrome is a bad thing – not least because, if unchecked, it can create stifling anxiety and a fear of failure.

But the fact that even the most successful people suffer from it tells you something important: you can live with imposter syndrome. It's not something you can conquer entirely, but you can learn to deal with it. And even if you never quite lose it, you can take steps to ensure that it doesn't knock you off course. Yes, Sheryl Sandberg and Michelle Obama are among the millions of women who suffer to a degree from this condition, but they haven't allowed it to impede their progress.

Understanding the Problem

Before you learn to deal with imposter syndrome, it's necessary to understand the problem and the underlying psychology.

The concept was introduced relatively recently – in 1978, to be precise – by Dr Pauline Rose Clance and Dr Suzanne Imes, in an academic article entitled 'The Imposter Phenomenon in High Achieving Women: Dynamics and Therapeutic Intervention'.

The two psychologists had spoken to 150 women – all of them recognized as high achievers, professionally and academically. What Clance and Imes discovered was that the participants in the study had a tendency to attribute their success to luck, or their abilities being overestimated by colleagues. In other words, the women weren't taking full ownership of their achievements. They were attributing them to external factors – those outside their control.

Basing their analysis on these interviews, Clance and Imes defined the 'imposter phenomenon' in terms of self-perceived phoniness.

Imposter Syndrome and Women

The imposter phenomenon was a concept that struck a chord. Under normal circumstances, scientific papers don't tend to pick up too much traction outside the academic community. But Clance and Imes's research put a name to something that many people had experienced.

When the two psychologists published their original research, they were working on the assumption that the patterns characterizing imposter syndrome were most common among women. This imbalance between the sexes was, they suggested, probably down to a range of factors – including gender stereotyping, family dynamics and even neurosis.

So how does that play out? Well, in a culture that places lower expectations on women, gender stereotyping can be internalized by women and so shape their attitude to success and achievement. At a subconscious level, a woman takes on board the message that society expects less of her than it does of her male peers, and this may lead her to think that her achievement is simply down to luck. And although it is rarer now than it was at the time of Clance and Imes's research, this kind of conditioning can also be reinforced within families.

According to Facebook's chief operating officer Sheryl Sandberg, men and women still tend to respond differently when questioned about their achievements. 'Ask a man to explain his success and he will typically credit his own innate qualities and skills. Ask a woman the same question and she will attribute her success to external factors, insisting she did well because she "worked really hard", or "got lucky", or "had help from others",' she said in her book, *Lean In*.

So, is imposter syndrome just a female issue, then? Not something that the other half of the population should be concerned with? Not quite. It's probably fairer to say that while women seem to be more affected by it than men, it's by no means a gender-exclusive phenomenon.

Men Feel Like Imposters Too

According to research published by Jaruwan Sakulku in the *International Journal of Behavioral Science*, around 70 per cent of people have experienced imposter syndrome. Research by training company The Hub came to a similar conclusion when it conducted a study with 1,000 UK adults. Around 85 per cent said they felt inadequate or incompetent at work, which included 80 per cent of men; 25 per cent thought their success was down to luck, and 15 per cent believed they had only got a job or promotion because of a shortage of candidates.

No one should be afraid to question their own performance – that's how you make improvements, after all – but persistent self-doubt is another matter entirely. Intrusive thoughts such as these may undermine your sense of what you can achieve.

Stop Feeling Like an Imposter

An individual wrestling with acute imposter syndrome can't quite believe that their success is in any way deserved. Typically, they will find it difficult to accept praise or any other kind of positive feedback. For instance, let's say someone comes up to them and says, 'Hey, you've done a great job.' Instead of saying thank you, they will look uncomfortable and say something along the lines of 'I just got lucky, really.' To others, this might present as a rather charming humility. However, in many cases, the reluctance to receive praise reflects deep-seated inner doubts.

In some societies, and indeed some families, self-deprecation after a compliment is seen almost as good manners – the opposite of boastfulness. In others, individuals are expected to celebrate and acknowledge success. But there is evidence that a reluctance to accept praise is linked to low self-esteem. This was the theme of a recent study in the *Journal of Experimental Social Psychology*, in which researchers David Kille, Richard Eibach, Joanne Wood and John Holmes presented evidence that people with a low opinion of themselves not only have trouble accepting a compliment but also struggle to capitalize on praise.

Why is this a problem? Well, normally success results in greater confidence. The more success an individual achieves, the higher their levels of self-assurance and job satisfaction. However, those who don't acknowledge the part they've played in their own success don't see their confidence grow in the same way. What can happen is that each personal or business triumph results in a growing fear of failure and a sense that their secret inadequacy will be discovered – possibly imminently. And this can lead to self-handicapping behaviour, such as finding excuses not to succeed.

A Hidden Problem

One of the great problems associated with imposter syndrome is that relatively few people know they suffer from it. That study by The Hub found that only 25 per cent of participants were aware of the concept, although most had at one time or another experienced it.

EXERCISE:

Are You Affected by Imposter Syndrome?

Ask yourself the following questions:

1. Do I succeed in tasks having previously felt I would not do well?
2. Do I feel like I won't be able to live up to the expectations of others?
3. Do I feel that I have achieved success or my present position just through being in the right place at the right time or knowing the right people?
4. Am I afraid that people may find out I am not as capable as they think?
5. Do I remember incidents where I have not done my best more vividly than I recall my successes?
6. Do I find it hard to accept praise?
7. Do I feel that my success is down to luck and not skill or talent?
8. Am I disappointed by my achievements?
9. Do I worry that people will discover how much knowledge I lack?

10. Do I tend to compare myself with others, feeling like I am less intelligent?

Score yourself between 1 and 5 on each of these (1 = not at all or almost never; 2 = occasionally; 3 = somewhat regularly; 4 = more often than not; 5 = constantly). Scores of 20 or above suggests some degree of imposter syndrome. Above 40, it is very intense.*

Perfectionists and Geniuses

When we begin to look more closely at imposter syndrome, it quickly becomes apparent that it is actually quite a complicated and multi-stranded phenomenon that affects people in many different ways.

Psychologist and imposter syndrome expert Valerie Young has identified a number of behaviour patterns associated with the phenomenon. She separates them into the following personas or 'competence types':

- The perfectionist
- The natural genius
- The expert
- The soloist
- The superwoman/superman

At first glance, these categories don't appear to represent attributes that are particularly negative or self-handicapping. After all, what's not to like about being a perfectionist, or indeed a natural genius? And isn't expertise a much-prized quality?

But as we take a closer look, we'll see how they dovetail with the imposter effect.

* Based on the Clance IP Scale, https://paulineroseclance.com/pdf/IPTestand scoring.pdf.

The Perfectionist

A perfectionist likes everything to be absolutely right. Not 95 or 98 per cent right, but 100 per cent right. When perfection isn't achieved, intrusive thoughts begin to close in. Even if a project is a success, the perfectionist questions their own competence. And they will mull over a failure for days – or longer.

So what does a perfectionist look like? Well, they tend to set goals for themselves that are not just high (a good thing) but excessively high. The problem here is that they may well be setting themselves up to fail. And if and when they do fall short, perfectionists will worry even more about not measuring up.

Perfectionists tend to be control freaks, and for that reason they are often very reluctant to delegate. After all, from the perfectionist's perspective, no one can do the job better. And even if they do delegate, they are prone to micromanaging.

This is something of a hamster wheel. The faster the perfectionist runs, the more rapidly the wheel turns. The result is anxiety, stress and perhaps even burnout.

So, if you're seeing yourself in this description, what can you do to avoid the negative consequences? The most important thing is to try to get some perspective on what you're doing and why you're doing it. Mistakes happen – they always will, even in the best-planned operations. Indeed, they're a natural part of the business process and something you can learn from.

What's more, it's important to remember that there is never a completely perfect time to begin a project. So if you're a perfectionist, push yourself to start before you're ready. If you have a project that's been on hold for a while, force yourself to start it. Don't let perfection be the enemy of the good.

The Natural Genius

These individuals like to feel that everything is effortless. Whether it's sitting an exam, pitching for investment or preparing for a major public-speaking engagement, the 'genius' expects success to be an easy product of their abundant talent. So when the genius has to work hard to achieve something, a chasm of self-doubt opens up.

In common with the perfectionist, the natural genius sets very high goals for themselves and wants to get everything right first time. In terms of the baggage they carry, natural geniuses often have a record of getting straight As in school or excelling at almost everything they've ever tried. They were likely told at an early age that they were the clever one in the family.

All this contributes to a mindset that on the surface is brimming with confidence. That confidence can be brittle, however. When things go wrong, the natural genius has a tendency to be beset by insecurities. Their confidence tumbles. And not only that – there can also be feelings of shame associated with not performing well.

Natural geniuses are often reluctant to consider seeking input from mentors. Ultimately, the fear of failure experienced by people who fall into this category leads them to avoid challenges in the future and they won't attempt anything they know they can't do easily.

So, can you sidestep the pitfalls of being a natural genius type? The answer is 'yes', and a good place to start is by acknowledging that, no matter how skilled and knowledgeable you are, there is always more to learn. Perhaps more importantly, there are always people that you can learn from. Look at yourself as a work in progress. Someone who is always prepared to watch and learn. Decide to accept help, and find a mentor.

The Expert

Sitting not a million miles away from the perfectionist and the natural genius is the expert – an individual who feels uncomfortable unless they have gathered up every scrap of relevant information.

Typically, you'll find an expert hoovering up qualifications – certificates, diplomas, degrees, etc. – as they feel that they must always be on top of the knowledge and skills acquisition game. An expert may stay in the same job or post for long periods of time, feeling like there is always more to learn. Ironically – although this is very much a variation on the 'can't take praise' theme – expert types don't like to be called experts.

Now, no one would say expertise is a bad thing in itself. Acquiring skills is an essential part of professional development. But – and this is a big but – when combined with an imposter syndrome mindset, the constant hunger for new information and expertise is a perfect excuse for procrastination.

So, if you're an expert, you should perhaps try to think in a different way. Look at knowledge as something you acquire when needed, rather than an end in itself or a means of validation. And remember that other people have expertise too – co-workers and career coaches being cases in point. Seeking help is a good thing.

The Soloist

Meanwhile, soloists feel that unless they do everything (or at least the lion's share of the work) on their own, they will be seen as inadequate or phoney.

So how do you know if you're a soloist? Well, if you constantly strive to complete projects in isolation without anyone's help, you probably are. Indeed, you might well have a tendency to make it clear at the earliest possible opportunity that you don't want or require anyone else's assistance. One way to break out of this limiting mindset is to make a conscious effort to seek help from others.

The Superwoman/Superman

The superwoman/superman fears being found out as a fraud, and so this individual feels the need to work harder than everyone else.

The superwoman/superman stays later at work than any other member of the team, even when all the necessary tasks have been completed. And at home? Well, it's hard to settle. Downtime feels like a bit of a waste. Hobbies and indeed all non-work interests fall by the wayside.

This may look good for a while – after all, everyone likes a hard worker. But the truth is, the superwoman/superman is addicted to the validation that comes from working, and what other people think of them. The job itself and the requirements of that job are something of a by-product. What the people in this category have forgotten is that no one should have more power to make you feel good about yourself than you.

Uncomfortable Situations

Imposter syndrome can also be driven by very specific situations – notably, those occasions when you feel slightly (or very much) out of your depth.

For instance, when I was pitching to buyers for the first time, I remember walking into a room and meeting people who seemed to share a common language that I wasn't yet party to. Every industry has its jargon – and increasingly, every sector has its acronyms that are familiar to those 'in the know'. If you're entering those worlds for the first or second time, it's easy to feel like you don't belong when people are using acronyms such as COB (close of business) or EOP (end of play). Yes, these are simple things that you can learn quickly, but until you do, your lack of knowledge means you are out of the loop. These days, I'm confident enough to ask when someone uses an acronym I don't know, but back then it felt like a problem.

Sometimes, imposter syndrome is triggered by the newness of a situation. For instance, when Byron began to bank with Coutts, it felt like an achievement. Operating as a private bank, Coutts offers its services to high-net-worth individuals and entrepreneurs, and it is highly selective about its customer base. Being accepted as a client is an indicator of success.

But as Byron admits, it was also daunting: 'When I began to bank there, I felt 100 per cent that I didn't deserve to be there. It's the Queen's bank. I did feel like a fraud.' And the other customers didn't necessarily help. 'At one point, a lady asked me what I was doing there.'

These are, first and foremost, uncomfortable situations that throw up many of the same feelings as imposter syndrome. They don't necessarily result in psychological patterns that become embedded over the longer term. However, they can influence your thinking, unless you remain self-aware.

Overcoming Imposter Syndrome

Which brings us to the question of how you can overcome the negative outcomes that stem from imposter syndrome. We've already looked at how the syndrome manifests in terms of specific behaviours, but no matter whether you're an expert, a soloist, a superwoman/superman, a natural genius or a perfectionist, there are some broad strategies you can adopt.

First of all, here's the good news: imposter syndrome is a mindset that marks you out either as a high achiever, or someone who has the ambition and potential to make an impact on the world. The imposter phenomenon is a response to achievement, so it's worth reminding yourself that you are an achiever. Give yourself a pat on the back.

And after you've done that, it's time to face the facts. There isn't a magic potion that will rid you of all those difficult and sometimes intrusive thoughts. That's why – as we've seen – Sheryl Sandberg and countless others say they still have days when they feel like imposters.

But there are some simple things you can do to help.

See What's Real

Try to look at the world as it is, rather than listening to the part of your brain that delights in being a critic. Separate feelings from fact. Maybe you feel like a fraud, maybe you feel stupid. Just because you're having those feelings, it doesn't mean that you are either of those things.

Be kind to yourself and look at what you've achieved. Starting a business. Winning a major new client. Securing investment. Think also of the people you've employed. The mark you've made on the world.

The reality of the situation is that none of these things – not one – was a product of luck. You wouldn't, for example, win an order to supply a major supermarket chain unless you had created a product the buyer thought they could sell. Yes, maybe you got lucky meeting the buyer at a networking event, but that's only one small element in the sales process. No one would buy from you if they didn't trust the product. And remember, you made a decision to attend that networking event. Your presence there had nothing to do with random good fortune.

Build a Community and 'Fess Up

Building a community around yourself is a hugely effective way to deal with the psychological issues associated with leadership. It's often said that running a company is a very lonely job. You may be surrounded by staff and senior managers, but there are often very few people with whom you can share your thoughts and talk through problems. Perhaps none at all. The solution is to create a support system – a personal boardroom of people you've chosen to help you on your journey.

The chances are that at least some of your circle will have experienced imposter syndrome themselves. So don't hold back. 'Fess up. Tell the people you trust and respect how you're feeling. This will help you to put a name to the problem and identify it as a phenomenon that others also experience. It's a 'thing' and there are well-documented patterns of behaviour and outcomes. It then becomes something you can address.

It's also worth remembering that all of us have our own strengths and weaknesses – or, in the context of a business, there are tasks we perform well and others we struggle with. One factor that may allow imposter syndrome to take root is the knowledge that, while a particular part of a project has been hugely successful, another aspect has been hit by failure. In that kind of situation, it's all too easy to blame yourself and think that the problems are down to a lack of ability on your part.

Next time, focus on your strengths, and outsource aspects of the operation you might struggle with. Get rid of the things you hate or – let's be honest – those you feel you don't do well. 'Nobody is good at everything. I choose to focus on what I'm great at, and make sure that I'm good enough at everything else,' says Sarah Ellis of Amazing If.

By concentrating on your strengths, you can focus on leading the team. And it will genuinely be a team operation, with everyone contributing in their own way, according to the specific strengths they bring to the table.

There are, of course, times when your feelings of being a fraud or out of your depth are based on an objective reality. If you're new in a job and everyone else has been there for years, you're naturally going to feel out of place – like you don't belong. And you might even think that you don't have the skills or competencies to succeed in this environment. It's a feeling that could be doubly powerful if you are one of a relatively small number of women in an industry, or if you are one of the first members of a particular ethnic community to join a business.

Remember that this is a reality you can change over time, by gaining experience, acquiring skills and making yourself an irreplaceable part of the team. In other words, a feeling of not belonging may sometimes be a logical or understandable response – but it doesn't have to be set in stone or be that way for ever.

Look at the Big Picture

The modern commercial world tends to take no prisoners. And in a competitive landscape, employees are expected to excel at what they do. Business owners expect the same of themselves. But there is a danger of confusing a natural aspiration to 'be the best' with the pursuit of a perfection that is impossible to attain.

What do I mean by that? Well, let's imagine you provide a service to clients. You work hard, your team is committed and talented, and most of your customers are happy. But you get a complaint. A small thing perhaps, but it undermines the sense that you are excelling at what you do. It shouldn't, however. The trick is to look at the big picture and see that, for the most part, you're doing all the right things. Learn from the complaint and move on. Don't obsess over it.

But more importantly, listen to the clients – the majority – who are happy. Speak to them. Ask them for testimonials; and when they praise your work, accept that validation. That doesn't mean you're not paying attention to complaints. But you have to put things in perspective.

You can help yourself to do that by adopting a new approach to dealing with failures and problems. Don't beat yourself up. See them as a lesson.

Make New Rules for Yourself

We all have a tendency to set rules for ourselves – and perhaps they're rules that no one else is aware of. For instance, as a company founder, one of your rules might be 'I need to know all the answers'. Fair enough, but when a member of staff approaches you with a question that you can't immediately respond to, or a customer asks why a package is late and you have no explanation, you will begin to feel as if you've let yourself and others down. Another personal rule you might have – and this is one beloved of soloists – is 'I never ask for help'. But this means that when you do come across a situation you can't handle, you will feel a sense of failure.

There are certain rules and principles that you should stick to, but many of the unspoken rules we impose on ourselves are self-limiting. So tear them up and, if necessary, come up with better ones.

And while you're at it, write yourself a new mental script. Maybe a negative phrase – such as 'One day these people will find me out' – keeps bouncing around uninvited in your mind. Thanks to the way the human brain works, thoughts just bubble up out of nowhere – and it's very hard to stop them. But what you can do is create a different narrative. Every time that negative thought arrives, replace it with a positive one. For instance: 'Everyone who starts something new feels off balance in the beginning. I may not know all the answers, but I'm smart enough to find them out.' Eventually, the self-damaging thoughts will retreat. It's like rewiring your brain.

Another way to refocus your mind is to visualize the work that lies ahead of you and your desired outcomes. For instance, if you are speaking in public or giving a presentation, visualize your approach and the response of the audience. Naturally, they will love what you do. This is not tricking yourself with false positivity. What you're actually doing is creating a winning mindset. This is something athletes do ahead of a big game, and it works.

Finally, don't wait until you feel fully confident before starting a business or expanding your existing company. Put on a show. Fake it till you make it!

Self-Limiting Beliefs

A close cousin of imposter syndrome is the self-limiting belief. Essentially, self-limiting beliefs arise from negative thoughts that tumble into our minds, telling us that we are incapable of doing something.

Now, on the face of it, that sounds similar to imposter syndrome, but there is a difference. Imposter syndrome arises from achievement. Self-limiting beliefs can prevent us from even *trying* to achieve something great. They limit our ability to make progress in our lives.

Self-limiting beliefs and thoughts arise most often at moments of stress – for instance, when we've chosen to put ourselves in a situation that is pressurized or out of our comfort zone. We're looking for excuses to retreat, and the brain obliges.

The insidious thing about these thoughts is that they don't simply tell us that we can't do something. They also give us a reason, which might be something linked to our own personality. For instance, a person asked to speak at an event might start thinking, 'No, I can't do that. I was never good at presentations in the office, so I won't be good at speaking to a gathering of two hundred people.'

Equally, the reason might be to do with circumstances. You might tell yourself that this is not the right time to start a business, because the economy is still in a depression after the pandemic.

Sometimes, your unhelpful inner voice might point out physical factors – such as ill health – that could prevent you from achieving your ambitions. Ethnicity, accent or social background can also come into play.

To a greater or lesser degree, we probably all have self-limiting beliefs, but perhaps we don't recognize them as such. The inner voice that says 'you are incapable' might appear to be talking absolute sense. Worse still, that voice validates your own fear of taking risks.

If you're going to overcome this way of thinking, you need to understand a simple fact. For the most part, the negative thoughts you have about yourself are not rooted in any kind of reality or experience, but rather fear. Or at the very least, the obstacles you've identified are not as big as you think. And they are certainly not insurmountable.

Obstacles Can Be Overcome

At this point, you might be saying: 'Look, I get it – we limit ourselves. But some limitations *are* real. You can't wish them away.'

That's true up to a point. But what we see again and again is that even those facing the toughest of life circumstances can push through to achieve their goals.

Witness the story of Isaac Lidsky. When he was just twelve years old, he was diagnosed with a rare, degenerative disease – retinitis pigmentosa – that would ultimately result in him losing his sight. As his eyesight began to fail, it would have been easy for the young man to assume that his life opportunities were also shutting down. Certainly, he found the prospect of blindness terrifying, but thanks to the support of those around him and his own determination, he won a place at Harvard, studied maths and computer science and then graduated aged nineteen. From there, he went on to study at Harvard Law School, graduating *magna cum laude* (with great distinction).

Without downplaying the reality of his condition, Lidsky came to realize that the narratives around blindness and the limitations it would supposedly impose on him were fiction. As he told *Business News Daily*, 'I learned that the ultimate responsibility for my life and my limitations begins and ends with me. It is my responsibility to proactively identify obstacles in my way and to look for solutions.'

Lidsky has since built and sold a tech company, worked for the US Department of Justice as a lawyer, and is today CEO of ODC Construction. He remains an inspirational figure. Someone we can all learn from.

Blockages

There are a number of common self-limiting beliefs that can slip into our minds and block our progress. They include:

- *I'm not ready.* At one time or another, most of us have probably thought: 'I'm not ready for this.' This thought may arise when you're about to sit an exam that – in reality – you've spent months preparing for. It may prevent you from going for a promotion. It could cause you to think twice before quitting a job and starting a business.
- *This decision is do-or-die.* You are about to embark upon a course of action. In your mind, it takes on massive, life-changing importance. This in itself can cause procrastination.
- *Nobody will take me seriously.* This one – quite closely linked to imposter syndrome – is something we see quite a lot in our mentees. It is partially attributable to a lack of confidence, but there may be deeper issues of self-belief (or a lack of it) that need to be unpicked.
- *These people are better than or different from me.* It can be very easy to think that because you are in some way 'different' from people working in your industry, your ambitions will run aground. It might be because you are a woman working in an industry dominated by men. It could be a matter of age (you think you're either too young or too old) or ethnicity. Whatever the reason, you suspect you will be handicapped. And so your mind gives you an excuse for inaction.

Telling Fiction from Reality

Now here's the problem. In all of the above cases, the self-limiting belief may also be grounded in some sort of reality. You may indeed not be ready. Maybe the decision *is* just too momentous. Perhaps you won't fit in, or people won't take you seriously. So how can you tell the difference between a self-limiting belief and a deal-breaking problem? Or, to put it another way, how can you decide whether to press ahead with a plan or listen to your inner voice and hold back?

One useful approach is to unpick your concerns, as it's actually not that difficult to establish whether you are or aren't ready. Consider what 'ready' actually means. Have you got a website? Are your business cards printed? Have you got enough money? Is the product ready for sale? Have you left your job?

Maybe you have a product, but as yet you haven't quit your job. Does that actually matter? A lot of people begin their business as a side hustle and work towards making it a full-time occupation over a period of months or years. On the other hand, the venture might be something that requires more hours than you can currently commit. And what about the website that is still in construction – at this stage, do you need it? Potential customers will certainly look for a website, but would it be a deal-breaker if you didn't have one for now? Then there is the question of how much money you actually need. Maybe the money you have in the bank isn't what you wanted, but it could be enough to get you going.

But what if you remain fearful, or at least cautious? Try to remember that delay carries its own risks. Let me give you an example. Some of the mentees that Byron and I work with were recently preparing for crowdfunding events. There was a degree of reluctance – a tendency to say, 'We're not ready yet. We need to get everything in place.' But, encouraged and pushed by Byron and me, some swallowed their doubts and went ahead with raising funds. They set their sights relatively low, but exceeded their expectations.

Deathbed Regrets

There are also personal risks associated with indecision. Procrastination is easy in the short term – it allows you to avoid difficult decisions. But what about the long term? The business you didn't start, the job you didn't take, the road you didn't follow, they all become regrets.

I remember people telling me, 'Don't start a business – it's too risky.' So I asked myself what the worst was that could happen. And

I thought, 'Well, if I start this business and it fails, I can always go back and get another job.' I realized that, actually, very little that was bad or irrevocable was likely to happen.

That led me to look at things through another lens. What if I was on my deathbed, regretting all the things I'd wanted to do but didn't? That's a far greater risk than the risk of failure. Failure can be a teacher – you learn from it and it helps you grow. What does not even trying teach you? I would rather try than live with regret.

Rise Above It

Self-limiting thoughts are usually linked to fear. Fear of failure. Fear of embarrassment. Fear that you don't have the skills. And what do these fears amount to? Well, you can explain it with this acronym:

F – False
E – Evidence
A – Appearing
R – Real

So what do you do when faced with that false evidence? You can resort to flight (**F**orget **E**verything **A**nd **R**un) or you can fight (**F**ace **E**verything **A**nd **R**ise).

It's that second approach that will help you succeed.

Chapter Six
Build Your Network

'Networking is a lot like nutrition and fitness:
we know what to do, the hard part is making it a top priority.'

– Herminia Ibarra

You're at a networking event and so far everything has gone well. You found the venue easily, and because you arrived and parked well ahead of time, there was only a short queue for registration. More importantly, your reward for attending an event that you could quite easily have sidestepped has been a series of stimulating and relevant presentations, keynote speeches and panel debates. It's been well worth the journey.

But now you've arrived at the tricky part of the proceedings. The formal part of the day has come to an end and all that's left – as the programme puts it – is an hour and a half of drinks and 'networking'.

So what you're faced with now is a room full of people that you don't know. Some are standing on their own, nursing drinks and canapés. Others have already huddled into groups and are engaging in intense conversations. A few – the faint-hearted perhaps – are edging towards the door, and a part of you feels like following their example.

You don't, of course. These are people from your industry and this event is an opportunity to meet your peers and begin to build the kind of business and personal relationships that could prove immensely useful in the weeks, months and years ahead. That knowledge keeps you in the room.

The next step is to overcome your natural inhibitions, stride confidently into the main body of the hall and strike up a conversation.

It's a bit like standing at the edge of a pool, taking a deep breath and then diving in.

The truth is that most of us – initially, at least – find networking events to be difficult, and perhaps also just a little bit weird.

Let's start with the weird. A visitor arriving unannounced from a distant planet might well conclude that networking is a social activity. There may be a bar involved, there is probably food, and what our alien explorer will most certainly witness is the hubbub of conversation as the ice breaks and individuals form pairs and small groups.

There may indeed be a certain amount of purely social conversation, particularly when old friends and acquaintances meet up. But for the most part, what is actually taking place is social interaction with a purpose. Most of those taking part will have some kind of agenda – not always terribly well defined – in terms of the people they want to speak to and the goals they would like to achieve at the event. That might mean talking to potential customers, suppliers or mentors.

That sense of purpose creates a certain intensity. You might start a conversation and at some point notice that the other party's eyes are scanning the room, perhaps looking for a better prospect. There's a lot of pressure to retain the interest of others. And equally, you're looking for people who are of interest to you. So yes, it's weird. Not quite a social event, not quite a business meeting. A hybrid of the two.

The Conversation Challenge

Then, of course, there is the fundamental challenge of starting a conversation. Us inner-city folk are accustomed to erecting our own boundaries and inclined to respect those of others – that's why we avoid eye contact on public transport or in supermarkets.

In contrast, networking events effectively invite us to initiate conversations with complete strangers. For many, this is not a comfortable prospect. There are too many inhibitions to overcome. The good news is that – unlike, say, a group of people on a train – everyone at a networking event truly does want to engage with others in the room. Though that doesn't necessarily make it easy to extend the first hello.

Networking Is Essential

So why do we put ourselves through it? The simple answer is that networking is essential. A positive and proactive approach to networking is a prerequisite not only for success in business but also in many other aspects of life. As entrepreneur and public speaker Porter Gale has emphatically said: 'Your network is your net worth.'

Renowned guru Napoleon Hill, who published his self-help classic *Think and Grow Rich* in 1937 and died with a personal net worth of $1 million, had a lot to say about networking. In particular, he came up with the idea of 'mastermind groups', in which entrepreneurs and business leaders could get together to exchange ideas and share expertise and knowledge. He believed that networking was instrumental in his own success.

But what does it mean when we say that networking is your net worth? Or, to put it another way, what is networking really for?

At its simplest, networking is about expanding your circle. Now, most of us would probably consider that to be a good thing, but if you're going to make the effort to attend events – and more importantly, achieve the best possible outcomes – you're probably going to be looking for tangible evidence that this will be a productive use of your time. So what are the benefits?

Jump into the Driving Seat

In our experience, taking the time to build relationships and networks – either formally or informally – puts you in the driving seat of your business. And that's true whether you're an owner and/or founder, or an employee.

There are several layers to this. First of all, attending events and effectively acting as an ambassador means that you become the public face of your business. Equally importantly, as you begin to network regularly you establish that public face in the eyes of a whole range of people who may well take a close interest in you and your venture. And that, in turn, means that you become not only a point of contact but *the* point of contact.

Mutual Benefits

Now, it's tempting to think that the prime purpose of networking is to build the kind of relationships that result in direct commercial gain. It's not unreasonable to hope that if you spend time at an industry event, you will meet people who may go on to become customers or valued suppliers. Indeed, you might even measure the success of your networking in terms of the leads and, ultimately, the orders that those conversations generate.

But it's important to remember that not all of the benefits of networking can be measured quite so directly. Approached in the right spirit, networking is not just a great way to bring customers on board, but also an opportunity to create a growing community of advocates and ambassadors. These might be people who like you and respect what you do, without necessarily being interested in becoming customers themselves. However, they might well recommend your business to others in their circle who do.

Of course, that might not happen for months or even years, but it represents a very tangible benefit. Most business owners or managers have received calls or emails that begin with something along the lines of: 'John Smith – you met him at a conference a couple of weeks ago – recommended that I give you a call.' And this is a great way to start a business relationship, because from the first instant you know you're talking to someone who is already predisposed to at least consider buying from or working with you.

Business Intelligence

Another important factor to consider is the amount of knowledge that is on display at the average networking event. Consider a conference catering for an industry vertical. What you'll see around you is a mass of people who really understand the business they're in. They have intimate knowledge of the market and how it works. They're up to speed with the new technologies that are coming on stream. And they're probably also tuned in to where the sales and supply opportunities lie.

In that respect, talking to your peers at a networking event can provide a deep well of industry expertise and business intelligence. Equally, if you need a mentor or a business adviser, a casual conversation over drinks or canapés can point you in the right direction.

This is not only true of industry events catering to a vertical. Local networking groups – aimed at small businesses in a given area – are usually anything but vertical. Sitting around the tables in the upstairs room of a local pub you might find retailers, electricians, marketing specialists, plumbers, freelance salespeople, and many others. But there are still common factors. The plumber might need some marketing literature. A salesman might be in the market for a bespoke suit. The local coffee shop could be planning a refit and need specialist tradesmen.

In other words, commerce is not limited to verticals. By networking, you can learn a lot about who needs what, and when. Maybe you receive a good lead first or second time around. Or you might find yourself talking to an accountant, and get some good advice on the importance of creating a process for sending and chasing invoices. Or perhaps you recommend someone you know to refit that coffee shop. Then, a few weeks later, the head barista hears on the grapevine about some work in your field that needs doing and recommends you. What goes around comes around, and that is the beauty of what we might call 'networking karma'.

In other words, do as much networking in as many situations as you can. Certainly that was the advice given by Richard Branson in an interview with CNBC: 'To get started, attend industry events and meet key players; join regional business associations and start learning about local market conditions. Also remember that you can meet potential mentors at schools, clubs and business groups.'

Six Degrees of Separation (It's Not Just a Movie)

Those are small-scale examples, but the beauty of an expanding circle of associates is that the bigger it becomes, the greater the opportunity to access people that you wouldn't otherwise have dreamed of meeting.

Back in 1929, author and playwright Frigyes Karinthy posited the theory that no one in the world was more than six social steps away from anyone else. You might not feel particularly close to the British prime minister or the US president, but if you factor in a friend who knows a friend, you'll probably find that you are connected by a relatively short chain of social relationships. Karinthy's idea found new currency in 1990, when a play by John Guare called *Six Degrees of Separation* (later made into a film starring Will Smith) explored its implications. Karinthy wasn't a statistician or a social scientist, but his idea has stood up to scrutiny.

Now consider the business world. This is a universe where there are probably only one or two degrees of separation between you and most (or even all) of the people that you would like to meet. There is also something of a snowball effect. As your network grows, the pool of secondary contacts (people who you don't know but some of your friends do) grows exponentially.

You can see this principle at work on business-focused social media platforms such as LinkedIn. Once you have a few hundred contacts, try checking the profiles of some of your contacts.

What you'll probably find is that you share mutual connections or even suggested connections. More importantly, you'll find that they are linked to people you should be speaking to, i.e. third party connections.

And here's the thing. It's OK to ask your contacts to put you in touch with their associates. People who can help you achieve what you want. That in turn will give you an opportunity to develop not only a far-reaching network, but also a carefully chosen personal boardroom.

The Personal Success Board (PSB)

As we have seen, Napoleon Hill developed the concept of a master-mind group of people – mainly entrepreneurs and business leaders who meet to share ideas. This aligns perfectly with my own belief that business success is not an individual journey. There's an old saying, 'It takes a village to raise a child'. Much like raising children, building a business is a community-led initiative, requiring a selection of key stakeholders.

Even though our first book was entitled *Self Made* and we meant it in the sense of 'to become successful from one's own efforts', that doesn't mean that your network and stakeholder relationships will not be instrumental in that journey.

When we think of larger companies, they have a board of directors who act as a support system for the business by providing expertise, experience and consultancy to guide the trajectory and ensure the success of the business. As an entrepreneur, you will also need a team to support your vision across various aspects – namely life, business and future prospects. You can see this as your personal success board (PSB) or as a matrix of people who can help you achieve your goals – an entrepreneur stakeholder matrix, if you will.

There are nine roles within the entrepreneur's PSB, which in turn can be sorted into three broad categories. They are as follows . . .

Support Roles

Challenger – They will challenge your thoughts and goals, pushing you to look outside of yourself and to aim to do more.

Listener – This person lends an ear whenever you need it. They are a safe sounding board for your ideas.

Life Support – When all else fails, this person is always there to pick you back up. They give you the energy and courage you need to achieve your goals and go after what you want, even in hard times.

Change-Maker Roles

Connector – They may not have the knowledge or expertise you need themselves, but they can connect you with the right people.

Mentor – A constant in your life who has the knowledge and experience to provide you with the active steps to take to make your business work.

Expert – The go-to person in your industry. They have been there, done it and they can align your vision with the reality.

Confidence-Giving Roles

Brand Ambassador – This person is influential, and so they are the ideal person to advocate for you and to spread the good news about the amazing work that you do. They speak about you highly even when you are not in the room.

Customer – They are your target demographic. Maybe they were genuinely a customer who has now become more friendly, or maybe they're a friend in the industry who can provide you with the insight of a real customer. Their honest and helpful feedback will help you to push your brand forward.

Lover – The link between you and this person may be
    romantic or it may be platonic, but they provide you with
    the love, intimacy and safety net that you need in order to
    thrive in business.

EXERCISE:
Putting Together Your Personal Success Board

SUPPORT ROLES	CHANGE-MAKER ROLES	CONFIDENCE-GIVING ROLES
CHALLENGER	CONNECTOR	BRAND AMBASSADOR
LISTENER	MENTOR	CUSTOMER
LIFE SUPPORT	EXPERT	LOVER

Fill in the table above with the names of your personal success
board members.

There are some ground rules. One person can fill more than

one role, but ideally you want a minimum of six people in total. You want at least two names for each role. Think about if one of your board members disappears or cannot support you for whatever reason. Do you have other people who can provide that support, or are you putting too much pressure on one person to be all things? As you make your choices, also bear in mind that there will be some people who are a constant feature in your life and others who are useful on an ad hoc basis.

What you have now is a plan for a personal boardroom. The next step is to think about how you will approach them and ask for their time on your board. Here are some questions to ask yourself before you do:

- What do you expect from them?
- Why have you chosen them?
- How can they help you to achieve your goals?
- How often will you need help?
- Is payment required for their help or expertise, or do you want to offer it?

The Benefits of Networking

At this point you might be thinking this all sounds very good in theory, but in practice does networking really deliver benefits on a scale that will make a real difference? To answer that question, I would invite you to consider the alternative.

Let's look at this from a business perspective. You might spend time in the office, perhaps cold-calling potential customers. That can be a pretty thankless task – not least because if you run your business in isolation, it will be difficult to know where the real opportunities are. Often you'll be relying on guesswork rather than industry knowledge.

Some people might point to an inbound marketing alternative.

Essentially, this is when you advertise online or create content that is optimized to generate search engine traffic. This is an approach that works for some people, but by no means everyone. When I launched my consultancy, search engine optimization (SEO) marketing didn't really work for my industry. The fact that the business did take off and went on to be very successful was largely due to the power of networking contacts and recommendations. It was all very organic.

At the start of my career, straight out of university, I was employed by Accenture. They used a training company to facilitate early talent induction training, and I delivered several of the graduate inductions – scoring the highest points they had ever had. Which meant that when I started my personal branding business in 2012, I told the founder of the training company what I planned to do and they recommended me to the London School of Economics and to a major bank. Later the LSE recommended me to King's College London.

On another occasion, I approached someone from Santander at a networking event and gave them an elevator pitch about my work. That resulted in me receiving a call from law firm Olswang (now CMS Law), which resulted in a meeting and a booking. They have been my clients ever since. Again, it was down to a recommendation and the power of networking.

Diving In

Networking events come in a huge variety of flavours. Just to give a few examples, there are industry conferences with networking built in, awards ceremonies, round tables with invited speakers, and trade fairs. There are also less formal occasions – for instance, if you ply your trade from one of the co-working spaces that now pepper the length and breadth of most major cities, networking is coded into their DNA. In large open-plan offices, you'll be meeting others over coffee and in rest areas. In addition, many co-working spaces organize a range of events that include talks by successful entrepreneurs and weeknight meet-and-greets. Many villages and towns have their own networking events – often held in pubs – for local businesses. Added to that there are considerable opportunities to network in private members' clubs and other venues.

But remember, this is the twenty-first century, and networking online is also an option. In terms of social media, LinkedIn provides an obvious means to make connections and conduct conversations, either with individuals or groups. Twitter and Facebook can also be very effective. The Covid-19 pandemic temporarily shut down many face-to-face networking opportunities, but it opened others. Webinars and online conferences conducted via video-conferencing tools such as Zoom, Microsoft Teams and Google Meet came into their own. Admittedly, such events have their limitations in networking terms. In a managed webinar, there is often very little scope for informal conversation. However, some event organizers will set up chat rooms and forums where participants can exchange ideas. You might even find yourself becoming part of a global community.

EXERCISE:
The Networking Plan

Think about what you would like to achieve from networking. How might it help you in terms of your personal development, working life or business?

Now list ten events or networking opportunities that you think would be useful:

1.
2.
3.
4.
5.

6.

7.

8.

9.

10.

Wherever you choose to network, the process – you could almost describe it as the 'workflow' – is essentially the same. You receive an invite, you attend, you engage in conversation, ask questions, spot problems from their answers, and then follow up with the solution that you can offer.

The Right Mindset

A note of caution. To network successfully, it is vital to adopt an appropriate mindset. This is not just about overcoming any inhibitions associated with talking to complete strangers. It's also about being prepared to give rather than simply expecting to take.

There's a distinction here. You can certainly see networking as a form of marketing – given that marketing is a holistic process that extends from early research through to communicating directly with customers – but it is not (in our opinion) about a hard sell. It's about building relationships, rather than coming away at the end of the evening with a batch of orders or solid leads. There are professional boundaries in networking which are required to build a business relationship that is centred on longevity as opposed to making a quick buck.

Solving Problems

As you walk into that room full of strangers, you enter a community – albeit one that forms and dissolves over the space of a couple of hours. Everyone there has something to sell, but not everyone wants to be sold to. So, let's view it from another perspective.

A great many people in that room will be facing problems or challenges. You have an opportunity to help them address those issues. Equally, there are people in the room who will be able to help you with yours.

It's important therefore to engage with those you talk to, and to genuinely listen to what they have to say. Hopefully, they will respond to you with the same spirit. That's when the magic of networking really begins to happen.

The future of good business is in seeking out problems and providing solutions, even if the solution is not one that you offer. If you know someone that can provide that solution, play your part by joining the dots.

Preparing for an Event

One of the best ways to overcome any fears or inhibitions ahead of a networking event is to sit down and work out a plan.

That might seem like it's stating the obvious. After all, most of us – all of us, I hope – will prepare carefully before giving a presentation to an investor or ahead of a meeting with a customer. And we should probably even do a bit of preparation before an encounter that will affect our personal lives.

The same principle applies to networking. There are, however, a lot more moving parts. When you meet with investors, you're faced with perhaps two or three people. They may ask difficult questions, but broadly speaking you know what the agenda will be. Compare and contrast that with a room full of 50, 100 or 150 people. You might end up talking to 25 of them, and you won't necessarily know how your interactions will pan out. So is it really possible to prepare effectively?

The short answer to that question is 'yes'. The next time you schedule a networking event in your diary, ask yourself the following questions:

- Who is going?
- Who are the organizers?
- What do I want to achieve from the event – what are my goals?
- How will I present myself? (Take some time to prepare and learn an elevator pitch about yourself and what you do.)

Now you can begin to think about how you're going to approach the event. Once you know who's going, you can draw up a list of the people you most want to talk to. In reality, you may not be able to get a full list of attendees, but if it's a conference you should certainly be able to see who the high-profile participants are, including speakers and industry experts.

You'll probably already have known in broad terms who the organizers are, but what you really need to find out is who will be 'on the ground' making sure that the event goes smoothly. That will give you a point of contact in advance of the event, enabling you to arrive early and, hopefully, ask if you can be introduced to some or all of the key people that you would like to speak to.

And once introductions are made, having a clear idea of what you want to achieve and how you're going to present yourself is going to help you steer the conversations accordingly.

The Elevator Pitch

That's not to say that everything you say should be preplanned and aligned with a fixed set of objectives. That would be counterproductive. After all, conversation is a two-way street. But what you can be prepared with is your elevator pitch – a succinct, powerful and memorable explanation of what you do, how you do it, who you do it for and why. This is how you're going to describe yourself in the opening 30–60 seconds of a conversation.

The elevator pitch serves two functions. First and foremost, it allows you to set out clearly and confidently who you are. This ensures you make a positive first impression, and helps you to avoid stumbling over your words. People are busy and often have a limited attention span, so you only have a short amount of time to convey your message, inspire interest and get the conversation off to a good start. Second, because you've worked your pitch out in advance, you're providing the other party with a clear insight into what you do, what you are bringing to the event and how you add value with your business or skill set. In other words, the elevator pitch sets out why you might be an interesting person to talk to and engage with.

EXERCISE:
The Four Steps to Elevator Pitch Success

The best way to create an elevator pitch is to base it on this four-part structure.

Study the template below. Fill in the gaps. And when you've done that, you'll have a pitch that explains exactly what you and your company do – and most importantly, *why*.

I am / We are a ....
....
[insert company type / description]

that works with / helps / teaches ....
....
[insert / define target audience]

how to ....
....
[insert challenge / problem]

so that they can ....
....
[insert benefit / result]

Try to incorporate something memorable about yourself which makes you stand out. Think about using precise numbers if it helps to illustrate the extent of your role or the value that you can provide – i.e. you are in control of x people, had a budget of £y, created a cost saving of £z. But keep it succinct and positive, and provide clear explanations rather than using convoluted job titles. Fundamentally you are outlining *what*, *how* and *why* – what do you do, how do you do it or add value, and why is that of benefit?

Once You're There

Armed with a plan, you will arrive at the event walking just a little bit taller, buoyed by the fact that you know why you're there and that you've done the groundwork.

This is, of course, where the rubber hits the road. All the planning in the world can't disguise the fact that you're now faced with the prospect of starting conversations with people you don't know.

The first thing to remember is that, even before a conversation begins, you are already making an impression. If your body language suggests that you are open, positive and ready to talk, it's much more likely that someone in the room will proactively strike up a conversation with you. This is less likely if you look nervous, guarded or uncomfortable.

Of course, we've all been in a situation where we're standing in a room on our own while those around us appear to be getting on famously. And the more isolated we feel, the more likely it is that a creeping sense of discomfort will show up in our body language. At this point, it's all too easy to engage in displacement activities, such as checking email on our phone or showing a more than normal interest in the buffet.

But guess what? Displacement activities don't help. In fact, they can make you feel more uncomfortable, as you know you're essentially hiding behind a prop. The important thing to remember is that, even if you feel uncomfortable, you can take control of the situation – perhaps with the help of a few useful hacks we'll go into next.

Hacking the Network

Starting a conversation isn't that difficult. One good way to break the ice is to talk to an organizer, mention a few of the people you want to speak to (having done the research) and ask for an introduction. Generally speaking, the people who run network events are happy to help attendees make connections. That's not simply altruism on their part. They have a vested interest in ensuring that the event is not only successful but that as many people as possible have gone home feeling like it was a worthwhile experience.

Introductions are not always possible or on offer, but that's OK. A useful hack is to arm yourself with a few prepared conversation starters. They don't have to be elaborate or particularly clever. Most people at a networking event will have their own goals – objectives that they would probably like to talk about. So one good way of engaging is to ask 'What brings you down here today?' or 'What are you hoping to get out of this event?'

There are variations on the theme, such as 'How did you hear about this event?' Or you could effectively invite another attendee to talk directly about what they do. Try the question: 'What are you working on right now?'

It's probably a good idea to have a number of these opening gambits up your sleeve, not least because starting every conversation with something close to the same question will begin to feel a bit unnatural and uncomfortable after a while.

Forget about Your Job Title

One common mistake that people make is to simply state their job title followed by the company name, and assume that will mean something to others in the room.

So, what's wrong with stating your job title? Well, a title, even when followed by a company name, imparts very little information. You might, for example, introduce yourself as Joan or John Smith, CEO of Smith Communications. But unless your company is a household name, that in itself won't mean very much. It doesn't tell the other party what you do, whether you earned that title or conferred it on yourself, or whether your company has three employees or three hundred. And titles such as vice president convey no real information about your role or status.

Better to explain exactly who you are and what you do (this can be helped by your elevator pitch). Saying that you're the 'founder of a fast-growing communications and marketing company that works primarily in the fashion industry, using social media influencers to promote our clients' products and help them stand out from their competition' is far more interesting and informative. You've just explained how you add value. You've just told another person why they should speak to you.

You should beware of false modesty. How many times have you started a conversation – whether at a business event or a party – and heard someone answer the question 'What do you do for a living?' with the reply 'I'm *just* an accountant [or other relevant job title]'. This is not a good look.

It's always tempting to be modest. Many people tend to downplay their achievements or positions, on the grounds that actions speak louder than words. They feel they should be recognized for the quality of their work, rather than what they say about themselves. The trouble is that in the speed-dating hothouse of a networking event no one knows your work. They only know what you are prepared to tell them. Rather than describing yourself as 'just an accountant', explain that you're, say, a tax specialist who can save your clients many thousands of pounds every year.

Now, you may be lucky enough to be a speaker or a panellist. This is a good thing. The chances are that someone else will do your elevator pitch for you in their introduction. So don't blow this opportunity by admitting to a lack of confidence. Here's an inconvenient truth: when faced with the prospect of public speaking, many people start by making an excuse – just in case the presentation doesn't go well. You'll hear people say, 'Sorry, I had a bit of a late night last night, so you'll have to bear with me,' or 'Forgive the nerves, I'm not used to public speaking.'

Two points here. First of all, nobody cares if you've had a late night. Second, if you make a bad first impression, that can colour the audience's view of what you have to say. So walk and talk with confidence, even if you don't feel it.

And here's the thing – once you begin to project confidence, your hidden fears or nervousness will begin to evaporate.

Listen and Learn

Let's assume you have successfully started a conversation. What next?

The best way to build a sustained relationship is to listen to what the people around you are saying. What are their ambitions and their goals? What problems do they face? Once you understand their problems, you might be able to offer solutions.

And why will they tell you about their problems? Because you pay attention, and ask relevant questions.

Always show an interest in what people have to say – make eye contact, and perhaps nod at appropriate moments. Resist the urge to jump in with your own issues in a bid to empathize or put your experiences centre stage. For instance, if someone says, 'I can't get people to stay for more than a few months in my warehouse,' don't reply: 'I have the same problem hanging on to receptionists.' At this point, you're not there to discuss your own problems.

Instant Karma

So how *should* you respond to a problem? You might recommend a (non-competitive) supplier, an accountant or a training company that you know or have worked with. There's no immediate commercial return, but you're building up a stock of social currency. You're establishing yourself as a good person to know. This certainly won't do you any harm, and it could well pay dividends in the future. It's good karma.

What you don't want to do, however, is use up all your time with one or two people. Nor should you forget your own purpose. At some point, you will want to continue working the room. This can be another socially awkward moment. Starting a conversation can be difficult, but knowing when and how to bring things to a close can be just as tricky.

Knowing how to move on is actually a vital and underrated skill. As US broadcaster Celeste Headlee noted in her TED talk '10 Ways to Have a Better Conversation': 'A conversation is like a miniskirt; short enough to retain interest but long enough to cover the subject.' When it's time to go, it's time to go.

It's important not to appear rude. After all, if you've spent fifteen minutes cultivating a contact, what you don't want to do is wash away all that good work by bringing the engagement to an overly abrupt and blunt close.

This is where a new set of hacks or gambits come into play, following my golden rule of not leaving the person on their own. You might try one or more of the following:

- The conversation closer – 'It's been a pleasure to speak with you. I'm sure you've come here to network more widely. Don't let me keep you much longer . . .' – followed by an option to move on to meet others together.
- Introducing them to someone else.
- Asking for an introduction.

- Relocation – moving to an area that has more people, i.e. the food or drink area.
- Changing your body language – having a more open body language may encourage others to join in the conversation.
- Inviting someone new into the conversation – this can make the conversation more interesting, or it may give you an option to exit without causing offence.

Remember, you are trying to create a lasting good impression, so pretending you have a call or that you see a friend in the distance is not setting a positive tone.

Following Up

The glory of a good networking event is that you get to meet and talk to a lot of interesting people. In some cases, it begins and ends at the event. Perhaps you speak to a fellow founder about their experiences hiring a marketing director. It's an interesting and informative discussion you can learn from and take on board, but you don't necessarily need to be in contact again.

But in many cases, you will absolutely want to follow up with a call or an email. It might be that the topic you discussed – hiring a marketing executive – was very relevant to your own challenges, and on reflection you would like to talk about it more. Equally, you could be in giving/sharing mode – for instance, you might want to pass on the name of a useful contact. More fundamentally, if you sense a potential opportunity, you will want to follow up fairly quickly.

Now, in theory, this should be a simple matter. You've had a conversation that is fresh in the mind for both parties. Getting in touch to move things on a little should be the most natural thing in the world, but we can all find ourselves being apprehensive about taking that next step.

If someone gives you their phone number, you can safely assume they are open to being contacted. Yes, some people – perhaps even quite a few people – will give you their card (although others see this as old school now) or swap numbers out of politeness, but that shouldn't hold you back. As a general point of principle, once details have been exchanged it's absolutely fine to follow up, unless or until the other party explicitly or implicitly tells you otherwise.

There is a certain etiquette, however. We live in a time when communication habits and preferences are changing rapidly. There's a lot of research suggesting that, in the early twenty-first century, many of us are shying away from voice calls, preferring instead to be contacted by text, email or WhatsApp, or via a business network such as LinkedIn. Twitter and Instagram are also increasingly used not just for posting but for messaging.

The shift away from voice calls is understandable. When some-one rings you directly (and this is particularly true of landlines that don't allow calls to be screened), you're not really in control. Some-one you may or may not want to speak to has come into your world and you have to deal with them there and then, even if you're actu-ally quite busy or simply not in the mood.

So if you don't know a person well, it's arguably more polite to use a less intrusive channel. Equally, however, you don't want your message to get lost amid hundreds of emails or ignored because your contact doesn't actually use LinkedIn very much.

So, let's think about a useful sequence you can follow.

First of all, send a polite, succinct but informative text mes-sage. This shouldn't assume perfect recall on the part of the recipient. It's worth reminding them where you met and what you discussed, before suggesting that you schedule a follow-up call or just to connect on social media. It's also a good idea to ask a question – something that invites a reply.

The advantage of sending a text is that it is non-intrusive, in that it can be read and acted on at the discretion of the recipient. But texts also tend to get noticed, if only because the phone pings or a notification appears on the lock screen of their smartphone.

Not everyone replies immediately. Again, that's OK. The moment might not be right to respond, and as the day progresses, any thoughts of replying might well be deprioritized. Never assume that silence on the part of the recipient means that the trail has effectively gone cold.

Generally, it's worth waiting a while before getting in contact again if you don't hear anything. And next time, it's worth trying a different channel, such as WhatsApp. At some point, you may have to assume that the other party has no real interest in developing the relationship, but it's acceptable to make a few attempts before reaching that conclusion.

Timing Is Everything

So how long do you leave it before following up? There are no set rules for this. In most cases, it's not a good idea to pursue contacts with texts, emails or WhatsApp messages within minutes or even hours of the event. Many people will want to catch up with work emails or office developments as they make their way back to their home or business. Others will simply want time and space to reflect on what they've learned and who they spoke to before thinking about their own follow-up strategies.

However, you do want to follow up the conversation while the connection is still new. And there are times when it is important to act quickly, in order to seize an opportunity.

That can mean putting yourself 'on the line' to some extent. When I was at the beginning of my entrepreneurial career, I attended an event at which Emma Sinclair was one of the speakers. That was quite a big deal. Having started her working life at Merrill Lynch, Emma carved out a career in investment banking and then entrepreneurship, before floating her first company on the London Stock Exchange at the unprecedentedly young age of twenty-nine.

I knew when I heard her speak that she would be my ideal

mentor. This was a real opportunity to make a connection. So I introduced myself, gave her my elevator pitch and asked her to be my mentor (she said no, and that 'if she had £1 for everyone that asked, she would be on a beach' – we laugh about it now). As soon as our conversation concluded, I added her on LinkedIn and sent her a bespoke message. When Emma returned to the stage, she mentioned me by name as an example of someone who had the right attitude and the necessary qualities to succeed in business. She added that I had really impressed her with my quick follow-up and she was going to meet me the very next week. If I hadn't acted quickly, that wouldn't have happened.

The moral is you should never be afraid to make contacts, and you should always be prepared to make clear what you want.

Networking for Introverts

Approaching a celebrated individual and pitching yourself is not – you might think – an undertaking for the faint-hearted. You could, after all, be greeted with nothing more than a polite brush-off or, worse still, a blank stare. In reality, most people who have done well in business are open and friendly, rather than deliberately rude or stand-offish. But they are also very busy, and are consequently careful about how they use their time.

Whether you're starting a conversation with a peer or approaching Emma Sinclair or Jack Ma, it might seem that networking is a sport for extroverts. That those among us who are less outgoing need not apply.

But that really isn't the case. For one thing, extroversion and introversion exist on a spectrum. Most of us sit somewhere in the middle, displaying a mix of extrovert and introvert traits. In the modern parlance, such people are often referred to as ambiverts or omniverts.

What's more, the words 'introvert' and 'extrovert' are often misused. Introverts are internally focused, and can thus appear to be very quiet. This does not mean, however, that they are shy or socially anxious. They may actually be reasonably comfortable in social settings, but prefer to listen and analyse rather than joining in.

Extroverts are externally focused and feel energized in the company of others. They tend to be talkative, sociable and action-oriented. In a networking environment, however, they may actually struggle to make the meaningful connections that come from genuine two-way interactions.

Apparent extroversion or introversion can be affected by circumstances. A feeling of being in control of a situation – say, running a board meeting – may bring out extrovert traits in an individual. Something closer to introversion may manifest in situations that are unfamiliar or feel uncomfortable. More importantly, people who consider themselves shy, private or introverted can develop skills that are usually associated with extroversion. We've all read interviews with entertainers who think nothing of handling a room full of hecklers but who still regard themselves as introverted. As humans, we can wear various masks to support our endeavours.

Thus, extroversion is not a prerequisite for networking. With preparation, anyone can learn to work a room effectively. The groundwork that we talked about earlier in the chapter can be immensely helpful. In other words, do your research, arrive early and practise some conversation starters. And if you lack confidence, go to the event with a colleague who can provide moral support.

Introverts shouldn't feel in any way handicapped. In fact, extroverts can learn something from those with introvert characteristics. The introvert's greatest skill is their ability to listen and analyse the words of others. The hail-fellow-well-met business leader of popular mythology can sometimes be just a little too fond of the sound of their own voice to really take in the points made by others.

ENTREPRENEUR INSIGHT:
Building Business Relationships

As a self-acknowledged introvert, Sarah Ellis, Squiggly Career co-author and co-founder of Amazing If, says she approaches networking in her own way. 'Helen [my co-founder] loves meeting new people and has a wide network. She is very happy meeting people on Twitter. I'm never going to do that. I tend to form long-lasting relationships. You have to be able to sell whatever it is you're selling and build brilliant relationships. But we talk about networking as people helping people. You change jobs, but you can take people with you. People are part of your career assets. Start with what you can give. Put giving before gaining. Trust in career karma. When starting a business, think about how you are building your network. You have to make the most of your connections.'

'I started a whole side product on Twitter,' says Helen, confirming her networking abilities on social media. 'We got chatting, I thought she was interesting. We had coffee and started a flexible working network.'

She advises being curious: 'I'm happy to go to all sorts of events. I'm happy to meet a lot of new people. Have the confidence to get outside your universe. I'll talk to behavioural scientists and with large and small company people. I connect the dots.'

Yes, as an introvert you could well find the prospect of a networking event daunting. For instance, Sarah says she feels 'much more comfortable with one-to-one or one-to-a-few situations. But to be honest, most of us do – and it's a case of feeling the fear and doing it anyway.'

All of the Time

But how often should you be networking?

Really, you should do it as much as you can when you're young, relatively free of family commitments and hungry to make contacts – perhaps two or three times a week. Further down the line, that might not be possible, but you should still make a point to attend conferences, round-table events, and other occasions at which you will have an opportunity to meet with others. Indeed, as you become more successful, you may well find yourself being offered opportunities to speak, or to take part in industry round tables. By then, you'll be someone whose opinions and insights are very much in demand.

But as we've discovered in this chapter, you should look at networking as a conversation – and you should always be open to having a conversation and building relationships. Organized networking events are the obvious option, but there's also that lunchtime queue (networking opportunity), that coffee in the break-out area at work (networking opportunity), that train journey (networking opportunity), that wedding (networking opportunity) . . . I think you're getting the picture.

So be ready, always.

Chapter Seven

Manage Stakeholders

*'In an age where everything and everyone is linked through networks
of glass and air, no one – no business, organization, government agency,
country – is an island. We need to do right by all our stakeholders,
and that's how you create value for shareholders. And one thing is for
sure – no organization can succeed in a world that is failing.'*

– Don Tapscott

A stakeholder can be defined as any group, organization or individual that is affected by a company's programmes and operations. All businesses have stakeholders. All businesses are at the centre of an often far-reaching matrix of relationships with people who have an interest in the company, its products and how it operates. What's more, these individuals can also affect how the business performs and develops going forward. As such, it's important to understand who these stakeholders are, why they're important, and how best to manage the relationships.

Let's step back for a moment and consider the stakeholder relationships that are necessary for sustained success. First and perhaps foremost you have your customers. Then there are the suppliers – the individuals and companies who provide you with the goods and services you need in order to trade. Closer to home, your staff are clearly affected by what you do and they are also crucial to the well-being of your operation – after all, a business is only as good as its people. You may also have a business partner or a group of investors who have either lent you money or bought shares. Family and friends – a neat term to sum up your personal circle – might also have invested or be providing a degree of support.

The common factor is that all these people – to a greater or lesser degree – have a relationship with your business that is more than purely transactional. For a range of reasons, your stakeholders have a genuine interest in what you're doing and how you're doing it – not least because your business is affecting their lives or financial wellbeing.

Who Are Your Stakeholders?

Each set of relationships is different. Some customers care about you because you sell them what they want or need to buy. In other cases, it could be a hugely important relationship. If you run the only electrical supplies business in your area, there could be a significant number of electricians and contractors who would struggle to get parts quickly should you cease to trade. Equally, though, customers are keenly interested in the prices they are being charged and the level of service they enjoy. If dissatisfied, an important customer will be quite willing to put on pressure, and perhaps even threaten to move elsewhere. In short, customers can affect the way you run things by wielding their buying power.

Suppliers look at things through a different lens. They want you to thrive because they hope you'll carry on buying from them. However, they face their own commercial pressures and may well ask you to pay more (when you really don't want to), or ask you to pay invoices within fourteen days rather than thirty. But the relationship often has elements of partnership, in terms of working together for a common good. For instance, a supplier may encourage you to embrace new ways of working, such as integrating your procurement system with their invoicing software to create a more efficient supply chain. And the close relationship between suppliers and their customers can result in new business opportunities emerging. It's not uncommon for companies to buy out their suppliers, to ensure they have access to the components or materials they need. Equally, a supplier might acquire one of its customers to create a direct route into the market.

Business partners have an even more direct stake. In an ideal world, their goals and ambitions should be aligned with yours, but that's not always the case. A partner may be a friend that you've known all your life, someone you've been introduced to at a net-working event, a former colleague, or a serial business owner with experience in your sector. They might invest money, time, expertise or a combination of all three into the business.

It's a similar story with investors (who may also be partners). To describe the relationship at its simplest, investors have at least two goals. One is to see the business succeed (and hopefully grow), because that's clearly good for all. However, with equity investors – who take a stake in your company in return for capital – there is a second agenda. At some stage, an equity investor such as a VC or angel will want to sell their shares and move on. Investors, there-fore, will have their own timeline. They will take a view on how the business should develop and how fast.

Those who lend money – banks, mainly – don't care about exit timelines, but they do want to be sure they'll get their capital and interest repayments on time. They may intervene if the business seems to be struggling.

Employees have a massive stake in what you do. You pay their wages, so it's in their interest that your venture succeeds so that you can carry on making the monthly payroll. They probably also want you to succeed for personal and emotional reasons. It's more satis-fying and fulfilling to work for a business that is thriving rather than one that is struggling. However, in other areas, the interests of the employer and employee may diverge, most commonly around sal-aries or working practices. This is where things can get a little complicated. Your team is composed of individuals, each with their own strengths, weaknesses and working preferences. And they are motivated by different things. For some, money is the driver. Others are quite keen on money, but what they really want is more status or responsibility. And others may do the job because it's local, or because the hours suit their family commitments. The job of the owner is to manage this diverse group of stakeholders.

And finally, there are friends and family. Close family – such as spouses and children – may be relying on your business for financial stability, and that makes them stakeholders in a very real way. And of course, friends and family members are often early investors or partners.

Sometimes – well, more than sometimes – relationships with your stakeholders do go wrong, and you need to know what to do when this happens. So, in this chapter, I'll be taking a close look at some of the key relationships and how to manage them – and how to avoid discord, arguments and tension.

EXERCISE:
The Stakeholder Map

Sit down with some sheets of paper. Write down your key groups of stakeholders, one per sheet.

On each page, describe the relationship. For example, one of your key stakeholders might be an investor. So what is the nature of their investment? Has your stakeholder bought shares in your business, or is the financial arrangement a loan to be repaid over a set period? Is your investor a friend or family member, or a pro such as an angel? What are their expectations in terms of the return and time frame for the investment? And what are the arrangements for terminating the relationship? Go into as much detail as possible.

Then describe the impact your stakeholder has had on the business. If you're talking about a key customer, you might consider how much of your turnover and early success has been dependent on that particular individual. In the case of an investor, what funding has been provided, and what has it paid for to date?

Finally, write down what the outcome would be should the relationship go wrong. What happens if your key customer goes elsewhere? Would the departure of your sales director cause major problems? What would the consequences be of an investor exercising their right to be bought out?

These are just examples, but the important thing is to look at each stakeholder relationship in depth.

Why Partnerships Go Wrong

No one goes into a working relationship to lose. Nevertheless, tensions inevitably emerge, often caused by a lack of clarity or a misunderstanding that isn't addressed until the situation boils over.

Let's say you go into business with a partner. All seems well at first, but at some stage you begin to feel that this is not, actually, a partnership of equals. You're in the office and on the phone ten hours a day, and most of the client wins are down to your efforts. Your partner is much less hands-on. They like to focus on the administrative side, but don't seem to be putting any effort into ramping up sales.

Something is wrong. Your partner isn't pulling their weight.

But is that really the case? Let's take things right back to the beginning of your relationship, and look at one possible scenario. Perhaps you had a great idea and a load of energy, but very little money or industry knowledge. So you found someone who had both those things. And from your partner's perspective, it was the investment and expertise that warranted a 50 per cent share in the company. Meanwhile, you're doing your bit by hitting the phones and selling your vision to prospective customers. You've both brought something valuable to the table.

Here's the problem. You have different perspectives. You've taken on roles that haven't been explicitly discussed, worked out or agreed upon. There is no consensus between you. That has resulted in unnecessary tension or an argument that need not have happened.

The same problem – stemming from a lack of clarity – could apply to just about any stakeholder relationship. Your customers may be expecting one level of service, but you're delivering another.

A member of staff may be failing to adhere to procedures that haven't actually been spelled out. An investor might feel decisions are being made without consultation, but you saw no reason to consult them on what you consider to be a day-to-day operational matter.

Clarity Is Key

Thus, the first golden rule of managing stakeholder relations is to be as clear as is humanly possible from the outset about the nature of the relationship and the rights and responsibilities. Or, to put it another way, you should seek to reach a broad agreement on your roles and the deliverables that are expected.

You could end up with a degree of ambiguity here, especially if all you're relying on is a discussion or verbal agreement. After all, human beings have an immense capacity for hearing what they want to hear. So, ideally, you should have a contract. A document that states clearly what is expected of both parties. The contract should also provide a route map that will navigate the parties through certain situations.

For instance, let's say the business begins to lose money. This is not good news for anyone, but what if one partner has put up more money than the other and has, therefore, more to lose? Or perhaps one party is not reliant on income from the business and the other is. What you have here is a situation where partners are no longer in complete alignment. Perhaps one would like to sell up before the losses get worse, and the other would prefer to focus on turning things around.

This could not only be a source of resentment, it could also paralyse the business. If two founders are pulling in different directions, it will become almost impossible to make the necessary decisions. A well-drafted partners contract, however, will essentially lay out the procedures for resolving the dispute. In doing so, it takes the emotional heat out of the situation.

Essentially, this partnership agreement enables the relationship to be managed according to accepted principles.

In the case of a partnership, a typical contract will contain:

- An agreed formula for the contributions of the partners, in terms of the money, time and expertise that each is expected to bring to the table. Essentially, this lays out what each partner expects the other to do.
- Details of what each partner can expect to take out of the business, in terms of dividends or salary (depending on the performance of the venture).
- The decision-making powers of each partner.
- The management role of each partner.
- Instructions as to what happens should one partner leave the business or die.
- Rules for bringing in new partners.
- A dispute resolution framework.

Direct and Honest Conversations

Now, it's important to mention that every organization is different, as is every business relationship. A good contract should be preceded by direct and honest conversations, covering roles and responsibilities and the what-ifs. The agreements reached as a result of those conversations should form the basis of the contract.

Contracts can be daunting, especially if a business has been formed by two friends who might feel that drawing up a legalistic document – full of lawyer speak – will somehow undermine their relationship to date. But think of the contract as a stress management tool. It's an independent arbiter that you can turn to when disputes arise. It's a way to sidestep damaging misunderstandings.

The importance of the contract holds true across the spectrum of business relationships. A customer contract sets out what is deliverable (and when), and what the procedures are when things go wrong. The same is true for contracts with suppliers. Shareholder agreements serve a similar purpose to those between partners. And, of course, when you take on a new member of staff, their contract will set out the requirements and responsibilities of the employer and the employee in areas ranging from working hours to disciplinary procedures. Everybody knows where they stand.

All well and good, but what if you're reading this after the event? You've gone into partnership with a friend, acquaintance, or indeed someone introduced by a friend of a friend, and all of a sudden things aren't going right.

Well, if that's the case, you need to go right back to the beginning and have the conversation that you should have had months or even years ago. This can be a tricky thing to do, as the ambiguity within the relationship might already have caused damage. But you may be surprised at the response you get.

Bring It into the Open

Have you ever been in a situation within a relationship – business or indeed personal – where you know something is fundamentally wrong? More than that, you know exactly what it is that has gone awry, but it seems so sensitive that you don't want to raise it in case you destabilize things even further. You spend a lot of time wondering what to do – frozen by inaction.

Then the other party says, 'Look, we really need to talk about this,' and voices the same problem that has been worrying you. And you know what – it's a relief. Yes, the subject is difficult. Yes, it may even be sensitive. But now it's out in the open, and that means you can find your way to a solution.

So, don't be afraid to reach out to a stakeholder – whether that's a partner or anyone else – and ask a difficult or searching question. You might well find that they are thinking the same thing. Vocalizing the issues that are bothering you is always a good thing.

ENTREPRENEUR INSIGHT:
Fixing Friction Fast

Sarah Ellis and Helen Tupper were friends long before they became business partners. Having met at university, they pursued separate careers before teaming up to create their coaching company. But even as close friends, they are aware that frictions can frequently arise. 'My top tip would be fix friction fast,' says Helen. 'That's not always easy, because we are two people who value our friendship and we don't like conflict. Fixing friction means acknowledging that we disagree.'

Their approach has been to formalize what they describe as a 'feedback process'. Helen cites the example of a meeting where one partner says something that the other doesn't particularly like or agree with. In these situations, it's necessary to talk openly rather than let the problem fester. 'We talk every other day. We have developed a framework of feedback in which we talk about what is going well and what could be better,' says Helen.

You could argue, perhaps, that close partners should just 'talk' anyway, without having to formulate a feedback process. But as Helen points out, it can be all too easy to get annoyed with the other partner because you make assumptions that aren't correct.

To illustrate this, she mentions a project that she and Helen were working on. Both of them were editing and sharing documents, but the project wasn't coming together. 'We were working on different versions of the document without knowing. No one said anything, so neither of us were aware of the problem.'

By ensuring that issues are aired and information is shared, you avoid that kind of problem.

Your relationship with a partner is likely – although this is not always true – to be close. Whether it's just the two of you or three or four founders, you'll probably be working together on a day-to-day basis, with each assuming an operational role. Sarah stresses the importance of defining roles. 'You have to look at your own strengths and where you can be most useful for your business,' she says.

That can mean putting ego aside. Sarah and Helen decided not to be joint CEOs. 'We looked at the role and responsibilities of a CEO for our business and decided Helen was more suited. So you have to have the confidence to accept that you have different roles to fulfil.'

Investor Relations

But what about your relationship with investors – the men and women who put up the cash, back your vision and leave you to get on with running the business?

Investors often consider themselves to be the most important of all stakeholder groups, simply because they are committing their hard-earned money and, in doing so, are taking on board a degree of financial risk. To some extent, that perception is enshrined in the fact that, when it comes to public companies, shareholder value is seen as the key measure of success.

The dividing line between partner and investor isn't always clear-cut. A partner – as we've discussed – may prefer a back seat or arm's-length role, with an injection of capital as their main contribution. Investors – be they angels, VCs or members of your personal circle – may, in addition to shares, ask for a seat on the board and a say in the direction the company takes.

Some investors – and this may be particularly true of angels who have bought and sold their own businesses and are keen to contribute expertise and experience – may offer to work closely with you on strategic, tactical or operational matters as part of the deal. This can be incredibly useful. For instance, if you're developing a beauty product with a view to getting it into major stores, having an investor on board who has previously been down that road is a great way to open doors that would otherwise remain shut.

On the other hand, your investors may be adamant that it is not their job to run the company for you, and that their main interest is in ensuring that you and your team remain on course to deliver what you've promised – usually, the growth that will allow them to sell their shares at a profit. Such an investor may sit on monthly board meetings and expect a say when major decisions are taken. Other than that, day-to-day management decisions will be left to you.

That raises the question of how the investor/founder relationship works out in practice. What decisions can you (and your co-founders) make on your own, and what needs to be referred to your angel, VC or family member?

An investor will, typically, want to be consulted over any decision that fundamentally affects the business and its prospects. You won't need to consult on hiring staff. However, if you're hiring a key member of the team – say an experienced marketing director who will lead the drive to scale up – your investors might well want to know. Likewise, any change of direction – say a pivot from one market to another – will probably need to be discussed. Clearly, investors will have a direct interest in anything that affects their shareholding. If you're planning to raise more finance, you need to talk to your current backers.

All this is common sense – up to a point – but there are potential ambiguities. So, just as is the case with your partners, you need to talk. More specifically, you need absolute clarity from your investors in terms of what they expect from you, and what they expect for themselves.

Impact on the Business

Equity investment – through which the investor buys a stake in your company – will to some extent change the way you do business. For one thing, professional equity investors – particularly VCs, but also angels – are typically looking for an 'exit' event, a point at which they can sell their shares at a profit. To achieve their goals, they will either need to see your company grow in value or get to the stage where it can be sold to another business.

This desired outcome clearly has an impact on your plans. The emphasis may suddenly be on preparing the business for a trade sale or management buyout (MBO) over a broadly agreed period of time. Or the goal may be to scale up quickly, putting customer acquisition – which is costly – and sales ahead of profit, at least in the short term.

This isn't always the case, however. An investor – say one that falls into the friends and family category – may simply believe in you and be seeking a regular income from your profitable business.

The first thing you have to ask yourself about a potential investment is: 'How will this affect my business? What impact will the investment have?' Then you need to talk to investors about their roles, expectations and, again, what happens when things go wrong. (And what does 'going wrong' actually look like?) You should also be clear on what you're expected to deliver, within what timeline, and that you're happy doing so.

It's also worth checking out their track record. Who have they invested in, and in what sectors? If you can, find out – and don't be afraid to ask them – how successful their investments have been. You can always call some of the investee companies. Some VCs actually encourage this.

The Shareholder Agreement

Regardless of who you take an investment from, the nature of the relationship should be set out in the shareholder agreement. These contracts aren't mandatory under UK law, but they are essential.

The contract is there to clarify the commercial relationship. Friendships and family relationships in particular can go badly awry when things aren't clear. As we've seen with partnership agreements, the contract provides an independent reference source.

It's important not to be intimidated by investors just because they have the money you need. Remember, they are not – for the most part – backing you because of a charitable impulse. They are looking for businesses, like yours, that can deliver the return they want, either through the sale of shares or through income dividends. If they offer to invest, it means that they believe in your commercial potential.

That said, they may strike a hard bargain in terms of the percentage stake in your company they want in return for capital, so be clear in your own mind that you are satisfied with the deal. The key to both sides being happy with the outcome is an open and frank negotiation.

And once you've agreed, don't begrudge your investors. At its simplest – and assuming all goes well – they are helping you to achieve your goals. If, when the dust has settled, you feel you could have struck a better deal, view it as a lesson learned for next time. If you're really not happy, you can always buy them out – or find another investor to do it.

Team Matters

The people who work for you represent a different kind of stakeholder management challenge.

Building a team is one of the most exciting aspects of starting a new business. Yes, you can get up and running as a one- or two-person band, but taking on additional team members allows you to operate more efficiently and to grow. Many founders also enjoy the sense of building not just a team but a common culture – an environment where everyone is pulling together.

Employees are undoubtedly stakeholders, but unlike a partner or an investor they sit within a hierarchy. Or, to put it another way – they are there because you employed them. And in that respect, managing the relationship with employees is a matter of – well, of people management. It's your job – or the job of your leadership team – to ensure that your people are working well as individuals and within a team context.

That requires a certain degree of flexibility. Everyone is different – both in the way they like to work and also how they learn (which is especially important nowadays, as staff are expected to replenish their skills regularly). But when it comes to managing a team, you have rules – set out in the employee contract – and expectations that apply to everyone. These can cover anything from working hours to dress code.

As is the case with other stakeholder relationships, discussions about what's expected and required should ideally start at the earliest possible stage. The job description in the original advert or brief to a recruitment agency, the job interview and the induction – these are all points where you can begin to manage the relationship.

Then there is the question of how you get the best out of individual team members. This requires a degree of knowledge. Who are the leaders – the people who can themselves manage teams? Who are the team players? Who likes working – and produces the best results – alone and unaided? Who needs support to flourish? Who is getting on fine without too much supervision? How do you motivate a diverse crew?

Working to bring the best out in all the team members should help to create a happy and therefore motivated workforce, and this will prevent key people from looking elsewhere. But there will be times when you have to say goodbye to individuals. Not all employer/employee relationships work. And this is true for all stakeholders.

Don't Be Afraid to Say Goodbye

OK, so you've had long and honest discussions, which have been crystallized in the form of a contract. In theory, everything should go smoothly. There will be disputes, there will be discord, but these are things that you should be able to resolve within the framework of the relationship that has been mapped out.

Of course, it doesn't always work like that. For one thing, the contract might make it clear that the terms of the agreement haven't been met by one or the other party, and that in turn triggers the clauses that define how the relationship can be wound up.

However, the situation may be less cut and dried. Sometimes relationships come to an end purely and simply because the people involved are finding it difficult to work with each other – or because they have begun to drift apart in terms of goals and aspirations.

Let's say you would like to grow your business nationally from a local base, and this will require further investment. Your partner, on the other hand, is happy with the way things are. Revenues are strong, the margins are good and you each have a 50 per cent stake in the business. Frankly, there is no reason to change.

Maybe you did talk this over before going into partnership. Perhaps you both agreed that, after a local launch, it would be great to expand the customer base right across the country. But times change. Your partner now has a young family and sees no reason to take a risk on a growth plan that would be costly, cut into dividend payments and – crucially – might not work. You, however, remain ambitious. Despite early discussions, there is no scope for reconciliation. At this point, the best thing to do is probably to agree to differ and go your separate ways.

A great many business owners have experienced variations on this theme. In my case, I found myself working with a partner in a situation that – to me – was unsatisfactory. Essentially, the business was growing but growing slowly, and while my partner was a great guy I wasn't happy with the progress we were making and how he was approaching the job. We talked about it – and discussed what could be done – but the improvements didn't happen. In the end, I made a decision to terminate the partnership.

I was a shareholder, and I dissolved my shares to allow the business to continue to trade without me. This freed up time and mental space, and allowed me to focus on other things. Your time is such a valuable tool. If I had not made this decision, I would have wasted a lot of it.

This is very often an extremely difficult thing to do, but in this case it was the right thing – a liberating thing. And it's important to remember that these things are not, in the final analysis, personal; they are commercial. In fact, my former partner and I still have a great friendship.

There is nothing wrong with acknowledging that something isn't working. There is nothing wrong with saying goodbye when it's the right thing to do.

Customers

Of course, in most cases, you won't want to say goodbye to your customers. I say 'in most cases' because many firms do find they have customers who use up resources – those who require a lot of maintenance and/or personal attention, for example – but don't actually generate much revenue. In these situations, you may well want to carefully transition your energies towards clients who make you money.

If you do decide to part company with a client, it's important to be both polite and clear, while avoiding the temptation to personalize any issues that might have arisen. What that means will depend on the client and the relationship. If you have a customer who is difficult (always finding fault with the work and expecting a lot for very little), it might be best simply to say that the relationship isn't working out.

If, on the other hand, you're losing money on a client because you have underquoted for work and overestimated the commitment, you have an obligation to fulfil that particular job or contract. But when that job/contract is finished and another is suggested, you have an opportunity to explain that you're going to have to charge more. The client then has the choice of accepting this or going elsewhere.

Generally speaking, however, managing this group of stakeholders usually revolves around doing what it takes to keep them on board.

To what extent are customers 'stakeholders' in the accepted sense of the word? Well, clearly every customer plays a part in ensuring your business thrives. That said, on an individual level, some are more important than others – and it really depends on the nature of what you do.

For instance, if you run a shop serving hundreds of customers every day and sell low-cost goods such as chocolate and newspapers, the individuals who buy from you are stakeholders only in a very limited sense. If a regular customer goes elsewhere to buy a Mars bar and a can of Coke, it doesn't affect your business much. Nor is that person reliant on you. If, on the other hand, you sell software training courses and have three big corporate clients, then you are financially exposed by the loss of a single customer in quite a big way, and there's a degree of interdependence in the relationship.

So again, let's look at some of the key factors we need to consider if we focus on only a handful of key clients. What happens if the relationship goes bad? How will it affect the business? How do you know it's going bad? And what do you do?

Customer relationships can impact the business in a number of ways. First and foremost, you lose money. And if a big client bales, leaving you with maybe two others in place, that's a third of your income gone – which in turn raises questions about long-term viability.

However, if you have 1,000 customers and one of them has a really bad experience and goes public with it, you have a different problem, in that the reputational damage can have a knock-on effect. Just one or two unhappy buyers can create a lot of negative feedback.

One way to deal with this is to maintain consistently high levels of customer service. For instance, when Bianca Miller London receives complaints about a product or delivery, there is a no-questions-asked redress policy. We send them the product again, no quibbling. It's an approach that keeps negative feedback to a minimum, although care has to be taken to prevent buyers from abusing the guarantee.

But what about those customers who haven't complained – how are they feeling? In my experience, the best thing you can do is reach out to them. Ask them if they're happy – and if they aren't, what would make them happy? It's a case of communicating, eliciting feedback and then serving your customers better.

Every stakeholder relationship is different, of course, but the common factor is a need for communication, honest dialogue, and agreement on what can and should be delivered. And that should be backed up by the agreement or contract that defines the relationship.

Chapter Eight

Keep Your Love Life

'We've just gotten to a point in life where Bill and I can both laugh about more things. And, believe me, I can remember some days that were so incredibly hard in our marriage where you thought, "Can I do this?"'

– Melinda Gates

Melinda Gates couldn't have been clearer. It wasn't always easy being married to the young Bill Gates. In an interview with the *Sunday Times* in 2019, she spoke candidly about her husband's struggle to establish a work-life balance at a time when he habitually worked sixteen-hour days. Eventually, time caught up with them, and, as we saw in 2021, their marriage unfortunately came to an end.

The truth is that starting and running a business can drive a coach and horses through the personal lives of entrepreneurs and their partners. I'm not saying that it always will, but it can if you aren't aware of the potential problems and don't pay attention to the needs of your partner.

No one is as affected by the performance of your business as the person you share your life with. It's partly a matter of financial wellbeing. If the business doesn't do well, there will be less money coming into the household – that much is apparent. But there's much more to it than that. The hours you spend at the office can impact negatively on the strength of your relationship, as can the stresses and strains you bring home after a rough day, week or month at work. Intimacy, sex, and your ability to talk, laugh and share good times together can all be affected by a failure to resolve the work-life equation.

And here's what you need to know. If you've chosen to share your life with someone, the chances are that one of your primary reasons for starting a business is to build something that will enable the lifestyle you both aspire to and the dreams you share. So, if your entrepreneurship begins – in any way – to undermine your relationship, then you risk a very personal kind of failure, even if the venture itself is a rip-roaring success.

That's why giving your relationship all the attention it needs and deserves is one of the most important things you can do as an entrepreneur.

Romantic Partnerships

There is, of course, no single relationship template – all romantic partnerships have their own dynamic. And when you begin to look at how entrepreneurship – or to be more precise, your decision to start and run a company – maps on to the life you share with a significant other, there are literally dozens of scenarios. We can't cover them all, but let's have a look at some of the most common situations.

One In, One Out

In this scenario – and I'm leading with it because it's probably the most common – two long-term partners are in paid employment and climbing the corporate ladder. They are financially secure, have a decent disposable income, and life is good. At some point, one of the two sees an opportunity to pursue a long-held dream of becoming an entrepreneur. This may come as no surprise to their partner, but equally the statement of intent – 'Darling, I'm going to start a business' – could be a bolt from the blue.

Whether a surprise or not, the relationship is entering uncharted territory. One partner goes to work as always, while the other takes over a spare bedroom (or dining table) with phones and computer, and sets about creating something from scratch. There is no guarantee of success. There is a lot of risk that wasn't there before. The status quo has changed.

A Double Life

Like-minded people frequently attract each other, so it's not surprising that many couples share an aspiration to be business owners – either in partnership with each other or separately. This can play out in different ways. If a decision is made to work together, the couple's personal and business lives will be bound together more closely than ever before. This could be a wonderful thing, or it could bring a host of differences to the surface.

If they're running separate businesses, they could have a situation where one partner is doing well and the other not so much. As a result, their financial contributions will be different – and this has the potential to create misunderstandings and tensions. What's more, their lives may run on different timelines. For instance, if one partner is keeping shop hours and coming home in the evening every day, and the other is frequently away on business trips or working late into the evening.

Someone New

Then, of course, there are new relationships. OK, as an entrepreneur you may be habitually working sixteen hours a day, but that doesn't mean you won't meet and enter into relationships with new people. If a relationship is relatively casual, your long days probably won't cause too many problems. As things develop, however, there is a danger that the entrepreneur's laser focus on creating a great business will begin to cause friction. 'You spend too much time in the office and not enough with me' is a frequent complaint from relatively new partners.

Watershed Moments

Even when couples are fully aligned and supportive of each other, there usually comes a time when it becomes important – actually, vital – to discuss what the entrepreneurial activity of one or both partners means for the relationship. You might meet someone, spend time together and, at first, it doesn't really matter what either of you does for a living. You're just enjoying each other's company and having good times. But things tend to change as the relationship deepens. That was certainly the case with Bianca and me.

When we met, Bianca was still at university and I had launched my first business, Future Homes. At that point, the success or failure of the company wouldn't have affected Bianca in any way. She was incredibly supportive, but she was at university living her own life.

Bianca continued to offer support when Future Homes failed, to the point of helping me set up another business and even doing the training to help deliver energy performance certificates, one of the key services we provided. We were a strong, mutually supportive couple, but neither of us was dependent on the other in terms of financial wellbeing.

That didn't really change until we bought a flat together. Bianca was in full-time employment initially, but then she decided to start her own business. 'That was when our lives began to really become intertwined. At that point, we had to talk about some real financial issues – not least would we each be happy to pick up the bills if either of us couldn't put in our half,' Bianca recalls.

Our experience illustrates just one of the watershed moments in which couples realize that starting a business has implications – in this case, financial – for their relationship. A moment when you realize that it's not only good to talk, it's essential.

Now, it shouldn't come as any surprise that it's a good idea for couples to talk about issues around work and finance. That principle holds true if – for example – you're both employees earning different incomes. In that situation, you'll probably need to discuss how that income differential will play out in terms of paying bills, saving for holidays or buying a house. You can see it as a sharing out of responsibilities according to the situation and the means.

And as things develop, circumstances will likely change. For instance, the arrival of children will add costs, while very often affecting the earning power of one or both of you. Again, it all needs to be talked through if the relationship is to be successful.

So are things really any different when entrepreneurship enters the picture? The short answer is 'yes'. For one thing, any decision by one or both partners to start a business has the potential to change the dynamic of the relationship, often in quite complicated ways. Let's say one partner quits a nine-to-five job to follow an entrepreneurial dream. Financially, things could be tough to begin with, with the newly minted company bringing in a lot less money than the paid employment that preceded it. That alone can put a strain on the relationship.

Roles also shift. If one partner continues to be an employee of another business, they may become the main breadwinner for a while. That could be fine, or it could be a source of stress, anxiety or resentment – especially if the new business doesn't take off. Protracted stresses frequently undermine relationships that previously seemed rock solid.

To give a couple of mundane but very real and present examples, there could be arguments over who does the housework or pays the council tax. And this won't do anything (positive) for a couple's sex life or the broader bonds of intimacy between them.

OK, let's pause for breath. The aim of this chapter is not to put you off starting a business by suggesting that it is a relationship killer. Quite the opposite.

What we really want to emphasize is that, yes, there can be relationship pitfalls. But more importantly, they can be avoided.

How Strong Is Your Relationship?

Every relationship presents a different situation – so can there be any common solutions? A good place to start is taking an honest look at the strength of the relationship itself.

Where are you with things? Is the relationship amazing, totally fulfilling and strong on every level? Or do you find yourself at the other end of the spectrum? Are you constantly on the verge of breaking up?

There is perhaps a greater likelihood, that you're somewhere in the middle. On a scale of one (breaking up) to five (totally brilliant), you could be on four, three or two. If you find yourself tending towards the lower numbers, you might want to ask yourself some searching questions as to whether the relationship will survive the stresses and strains of a complete change of career direction. Will you be able to work together, if that's the plan? Will one partner spending long hours on the business undermine a relationship that is already insecure? On the other hand, a score of four or five bodes well, but it doesn't mean that you should take the relationship for granted.

In a nutshell, you need to think about the impact that starting a business will have on what you already share. Bear in mind that one or both partners starting a business might ultimately have a positive impact. When an employee is unhappy at work, that also feeds stress into their romantic life. The same person – happy as a founder and CEO – may well be a better partner. But, arguably, only if the underlying romantic partnership is already sound.

Why Relationships Fail

Relationships fail for a variety of reasons. According to marriage counselling organization Relate, the two most common are:

- Disputes over money
- Sex and, more broadly, intimacy

Relate also warn that an inability to resolve conflict is a major factor, and according to research carried out by household goods manufacturer Vileda, 30 per cent of married couples split because of disputes over household chores – in other words, division of labour.

But aside from those elephants in the room, there are other factors – also named by Relate – such as:

- Lack of trust
- Differing expectations, goals and priorities
- Lives moving at different speeds
- Poor communication

We've already touched on some of the money issues that can arise, particularly when a business isn't going well. If we have an entrepreneur/employee household, the partner who is holding down a possibly very boring nine-to-five job ends up paying all the bills, while their other half is apparently having a great time going to industry events, schmoozing potential clients and coming home late, Monday to Friday.

But there's not only a money issue here, there's also potentially a trust problem. It may manifest as a lack of trust in the business itself ('Will it ever make a decent profit?') or worries about the entrepreneurial partner ('Is he or she spending too much time away? Are those regular evening networking sessions really doing any good or are they just an excuse to get out of the house?').

Then there is the question of different goals. Let's say you have always aspired to be an entrepreneur. OK, your partner gets that, but that's not quite the same thing as sharing the dream. In fact, what matters to your partner is spending time together and having enough money to enjoy life.

There's a divergence here. This can, in turn, lead to a feeling that each partner is moving at a different speed – or at least progressing along different tramlines.

So, you grow apart. And as a sense of alienation creeps in, there is a danger that both parties will become less open and upfront with each other – something that will only make matters worse.

Negotiate Up Front

It's a situation that Jennifer Petriglieri – associate professor of Organizational Behaviour at the INSEAD business school and author of *Couples Who Work* – knows and recognizes. 'You have situations where one partner goes into entrepreneurship and the other gets resentful,' she says. 'To avoid problems, you have to understand your partner's aspirations. In my experience, the couples who do best in these situations are the couples who negotiate before an event is set in motion.'

Every relationship is different, but these strains and stresses are experienced by couples of all sexual orientations and across cultures and ethnicities.

Agreeing on a Common Vision

So, before starting a business, one of the most important things you can do is talk about it with your partner and agree on a common vision. But what exactly does that mean?

You probably have a vision for your company – most entrepreneurs will happily talk at length on that subject – but that won't necessarily cut much ice with a partner who is following a different career or life path. In fact, when you think about it, staff members, customers and suppliers may be more personally invested in the business 'vision' than the founder's romantic partner. After all, they are living and working with it every day.

But that's only seeing part of the picture. What partners can agree on is the common vision they have for themselves as a couple. Essentially, this is a vision of what winning as a couple looks like.

Let's assume for the moment that one partner is focused on climbing the corporate career ladder and the other is concentrating on turning a business idea into a trading reality. In terms of their working lives, they each have their own priorities. Their common vision will focus on the things they share in terms of their lifestyle, and how the life they want can be achieved.

EXERCISE:
Common Vision, Common Goals

Write down your goals, both business and personal. (If you aren't sure how, turn back to Chapter Two.) Then get your partner to do the same.

Do this independently. Then get together and discuss what you've written. Find the common elements. These are the things you can both work towards – your common vision.

Elements of a Common Vision

What are the elements that can feed into a common vision? Well, expectations are a good starting point. What, as a couple, are your aspirations regarding income, the type of house you want to live in (and where), the holidays you plan to share, the cars you envisage driving?

It doesn't have to all be financial. This discussion will probably also include whether you want children (or not), whether you aspire to an urban or rural lifestyle, and who your peers are going to be.

You might also want to consider your vision for the relationship itself. How much time would you ideally like to spend with each other and with friends? Are you the sort of couple that likes to do lots of things together, or do you both tend towards quite a high degree of independence – not only in your working lives, but also in terms of hobbies, interests, friends and each other?

Professor Petriglieri sees this in terms of mutually agreed parameters. 'You can set boundaries [around aspects of the relationship],' she says. 'For instance, how much time do you spend at work? Is working every Sunday too much?' Essentially, what you're doing is laying down guidelines. So if a partner agrees not to work every Sunday but does so anyway, a line has been crossed. It's clear-cut, and this makes it easier to address.

It's also important to discuss what you need from each other. As an entrepreneur, you probably feel it would be helpful to have the support of your partner. But there has to be reciprocity. Find out what your partner needs from you.

Clearly, once you start a business, its success or failure has a very tangible bearing on your lifestyle. If it's not generating cash, then it's going to be hard to buy that five-bedroom house in the countryside – the home that might, in fact, have been in reach had both parties continued climbing their respective corporate career ladders. Holidays might have to be put on hold for a while. Shared interests might have to take a back seat while the partner who is an entrepreneur works twelve to fourteen hours a day.

In other words, once you've talked about and agreed on a common vision, there are trickier issues to address.

Uncertainty and Risk

What happens to the relationship if the business operates at a loss, or makes a profit that nonetheless falls short of income expectations?

Any decision to start a business carries with it a degree of uncertainty. You can't possibly know if you'll succeed. And it's not just the entrepreneur who assumes the risk, it's also their long-term partner.

So it's absolutely crucial to talk through the financial side of your business plan. It's only fair that your partner understands both the opportunity and the potential downsides of the business idea. And be honest. Entrepreneurs are often natural optimists, but your partner will want all the facts. If you're forecasting potential revenues and profits, offer up best-, mid- and worst-case scenarios.

You should also talk about timing. Let's say you make a decision to start a photography business specializing in weddings and other special events. Your business plan projects that it will take a number of months to get the word out that you're available, and perhaps the same amount of time again to build a customer base. Your plan suggests that in six to eight months' time, the business will start to snowball as your reputation grows.

To cushion you through the lean times you have some money set aside – savings perhaps, or a redundancy cheque. In addition – for a time at least – your partner can cover the most pressing bills. This timeline is essentially your plan A.

But what happens if the business plan proves to be over-optimistic? Maybe, after six months, you have some customers but not many. The number is growing, but not as fast as expected. You've put flyers through doors, advertised on social media and networked like crazy, but income remains low. Your partner is now the main provider, but their salary is not sufficient to pay the bills and fund the lifestyle you both want. Your partner is looking less and less comfortable.

ENTREPRENEUR INSIGHT:
The Born Entrepreneur

Mark Dixon is a serial entrepreneur who currently owns and runs the air conditioning company Impact PM. He is married to Gloria and is a father of three.

In Mark's experience, the relationship challenges facing entrepreneurs evolve as the business develops. 'At the beginning there is always a lot of trepidation,' he says. 'You don't know how things are going to turn out. As the business grows, time can be an issue

---

and you don't always have a lot of money, so that can cause problems. Further on, success or failure will have an impact. If the business succeeds, you'll have more time and more money. On the flipside, if it fails, there will be no money and no fun.'

Mark has been fortunate in that Gloria has always understood his ambitions and had confidence in him. *'She always says, if I have a phone and a laptop I can do something.'* But there have been tough times. Mark cites a hungry period after he was bought out by a partner. *'We had to live on savings until the money came through.'* When the cash finally arrived he invested in a tech business, which didn't succeed.

At times when money is an issue, Mark cautions against arguing. *'I believe you should apportion responsibility in terms of who pays for what,'* he says. *'If the other person can't meet their responsibilities, there is no point in arguing. Arguing about money is the road to ruin.'*

Mark doesn't think that starting a business is a handicap in starting a new relationship. *'In fact, it can be an advantage,'* he says. *'You have more flexibility.'* Children, on the other hand, can require flexibility from others. *'If you have things to do, you can't just set them aside to do the school run. You need a network for childcare. We were lucky enough to have the support of Gloria's mother.'*

He is sceptical about formalized romantic solutions, such as date nights. *'If things are going well, you'll have time and romance. If there isn't any money around, that goes out the window – no money, no honey.'*

The Emergency Budget

When you set out your best-, middle- and worst-case scenarios, harness your projections to an estimated or agreed timeline and an emergency budget – a plan B, to fill in the financial gaps. For instance, you might – as many photographers do – get a second job that gives you a guaranteed income for a couple of days a week.

This is the kind of contingency plan that should always be part of your initial discussions with your partner. To put it bluntly, it lets your long-term partner know that there is a way out – a survival plan – if things go badly. And that the way out is tied to a schedule.

The emergency plan – which could also include returning to a paid job after a set period – is something that needs to be regularly reviewed. You might give yourself six months to succeed, but what happens when the deadline passes and you are almost hitting your targets? Do you stick or do you fold? That's something that you need to discuss as the situation evolves.

The benefits of having such a plan are twofold. In purely financial terms, it is a route map out of trouble. But it is also a psychological crutch. It provides reassurance that the failure or underperformance of the business will not run your bigger life vision off the road.

Day-to-Day Money Matters

Emergency planning is only part of the budgetary picture. You should also be discussing how to manage your household and personal spending. This is something that you probably talk about anyway – regardless of whether or not entrepreneurship has entered the picture. There's no 'right' way to organize your finances. Some couples prefer separate bank accounts; others prefer everything to be in both their names. Various arrangements sit in between.

But here's a good way to think about the conversation. You have three pots for money, labelled 'yours', 'ours' and 'mine'. How does that break down? Do you put everything into the pot designated 'ours', or do you factor in a degree of independence by including funds in 'yours' and 'mine'? And this leads to a very obvious question. How much does each of you put into the 'ours' pot?

This is something you'll need to review when the decision to start a business is made and there is (hopefully temporarily) less money around. Two questions arise: How much money will each of you now contribute to household spending? And what happens if the money available in the 'ours' pot doesn't cover all the outgoings? For instance, is there money that can be diverted from the other pots, and for how long?

Which brings us back to the emergency budget – an agreed provision to ensure all the bills can be paid and financial commitments will be met, should one partner be falling short.

Financial Decision-Making

The financial recalibration that takes place after one partner – or indeed both partners – start a business frequently brings to the surface issues about decision-making within the relationship. Let's look at an example. A business needs to spend money on new computer equipment. It's a small company – only a few people at this stage – but the bill for several tablets, a number of laptops and a couple of laser printers comes to £5,000.

Ostensibly, whether to spend the money is a decision for the partner who is running the startup company. Actually, though, the upfront spending affects the amount of money that is available to channel into the household budget. So how much should one partner tell the other about the amount being spent on the business?

This is not clear-cut. Spending on stationery and small pieces of office equipment doesn't require a check-in. On the other hand, maybe £5,000 worth of computer equipment does.

More acutely, borrowing to fund growth is a business decision, but if the founder has to give a personal guarantee against property, then it affects their family should things go wrong. In extreme circumstances, a couple could actually lose their home. Again, in this case there is a need for a check-in. These things need to be discussed.

Now, that all sounds fine in theory. In practice, there are questions here about demarcations and responsibility. When does the entrepreneur talk things over with a romantic partner before making a financial decision? And when is it OK just to spend? This will be different for every couple, but it is something that should be addressed.

And in many ways, this is an issue that speaks to the personalities in the couple. Within a relationship, one partner might be a spender (always happy to make big purchases) and the other a saver (constantly putting away money for a rainy day). The spender might think it's fine to buy that IT equipment without consultation – after all, there isn't much money involved and it's a necessary business expense. Meanwhile the saver feels – and feels very, very strongly – that this should have been discussed.

In my own relationship, I probably tend more towards the spender side of the equation, with Bianca seeing herself as a saver. Perhaps there's a gender divide here. Arguably men – and I could be an example of this – are willing to spend more without consultation than women are.

Of course, it's perfectly possible that both partners are big spenders. That sounds like a recipe for harmony of a sort, or at least symmetry. Sadly, that's not necessarily the case. The couple in question might want to spend their money on different things. There may, for instance, be a divide regarding what is deemed necessary or acceptable expenditure based on associated value. One partner may think it's absolutely fine to splash out £1,000 or so on a designer handbag, while the other partner shakes their head in a certain amount of disbelief. Meanwhile, they're planning to spend twice as much on a top-of-the-range MacBook for the home office. Wouldn't a Windows laptop be cheaper and just as good, given that there are bills to pay and a family holiday to book?

Again, it's important to set guidelines. Each partner needs to know when they need to check in with the other about spending, and when it's OK to pull the trigger without consultation. When starting a business, any expenditures can affect the business and personal household expenses, so they need to be discussed and agreed upon to prevent further tensions.

Assigning Roles

It's a wet Thursday in summer, and Anna comes home from a difficult day at the office. Her partner Tom has also been working all day – adding content to his new website, and later composing a marketing email that will be sent out to mailing list subscribers. As he sees it, he's been pretty busy.

A row flares up. Housework hasn't been done. Anna feels Tom should have done it because he's been at home all day. Tom points to the fact that he's been sitting at his computer since eight without a break. Anna doesn't quite believe that Tom couldn't have taken half an hour to put on the laundry and tidy away the breakfast dishes.

This particular argument is not so much about the couple not understanding each other – although that can play a part – and more about the different perspectives that can emerge. Both have been working all day, but there is an assumption on Anna's part that a bit of basic housework could easily be factored into her partner's day. There is perhaps a need to assign roles and responsibilities. And it goes beyond who does the laundry. Who pays the household bills? Who does the school run?

Roles and responsibilities also come into play when couples are working together within a business. To some extent, each partner might do a bit of everything, but there is also a case for dividing things up according to skills or disposition. For instance, one partner might focus on the admin, with the other being the 'face' of the business, meeting customers and attending events. To be honest, you can both be the face (or faces) – that's certainly how it is with Bianca and me – but it's still a good idea to talk about roles. We certainly don't believe in duplication of work, and will divide responsibilities according to skill set.

It's worth pointing out here that when two romantic partners are working together in the same business, they are also – to state the obvious – business partners. And as the previous chapter showed, in any business partnership it's unwise to assign roles and responsibilities solely by verbal agreement. All business partnerships should be defined by a formal written agreement – even those that involve someone you share a life with. A formal document provides an independent template through which to handle disputes.

ENTREPRENEUR INSIGHT:
Defining Roles

In 2010, Yvette Noel-Schure quit her job as a high-flying publicist and senior VP for Columbia Records, with no concrete plans to set up her own business. 'I had no business plan and I did not envisage having a business plan,' she says.

But when Beyoncé rang up asking to hire Yvette as a publicist a few months later, Yvette's husband had a business plan ready. 'That was good, but what I wasn't sure about was why he wanted to have a role in my business. He was already running a successful business.'

The possible shape of the working relationship became clear shortly afterwards. Checking her bank account, Yvette realized there was less in there than she had been expecting. The reason? While being one of the best publicists in the industry, in her career she hadn't previously had to think about the administrative side of running a business, such as sending out invoices. 'A friend told me – you are good at a lot of things but not running a business. I realized then, I was married to an executive. It was a revelation that provided clearly defined roles. Me dealing with the creative, fun side. Him handling all the bills and contracts.'

Work Patterns

That's the work side, but what about the fun things in life? Relationships aren't just about who does the household chores; they are, more importantly, about the time you spend enjoying each other's company and doing things together. Remember that common vision . . .

One potential problem in this regard is the impact of new and different working patterns. We all have our own ways of organizing our days. Some of us are owls, some of us are larks. Or to put it more scientifically, each of us has our own circadian rhythm. For some, the ideal day involves waking up early and getting started on work before most of the rest of the world has even had a shower. Others are at their most creative and productive in the evenings or late at night.

If you commute to work and do a nine-to-five job, your natural rhythm tends to be overridden by the requirements of a heavily organized working day. Once one or both partners quit work to pursue an entrepreneurial career, the rhythms change.

First and foremost, the recently fledged entrepreneur probably finds that they are working more hours. That means having to find more time in the day to spend on the business – early in the morning or late in the evening, depending on when they work best. There may be significant time commitments imposed by the business itself. Working on Saturday or Sunday perhaps – or, as we've discussed, attending networking events in the evening.

This won't matter much if the couple are following the same working pattern, but often that's not actually the case. When they were both working nine-to-five jobs, they knew they could spend quality time together after work or at the weekends. With a new business up and running this becomes less simple. They might even find that they have to schedule time together.

If you're in a long-term relationship, the change in working patterns caused by starting a business can have a profound impact on your personal life. Any sudden contraction of the time available to see your partner can undermine your relationship in the longer term. Again, the best way to avoid this trap is to talk. If you are the entrepreneur in the partnership, it's important to explain how your working day pans out and why you do what you do. It's also important to make time for the other person. And if you're both entrepreneurs, have the same conversation. The business dream shouldn't conflict with the common vision.

But what does that mean in practical day-to-day terms? Well, think of the things that you like doing together as a couple. Going to the cinema, eating out, taking weekend city breaks, maybe skiing in the winter. You need to find time to do these things. Yes, for a while – as the business grows and money is tighter than it should be – you might need to cut back a little, with activities making way for 'Netflix time' at home, but it's important to sustain your shared interests.

Be Inclusive

Things might get a bit tricky if it appears that you're having an exciting, even glamorous life – one that your partner doesn't get to experience. Maybe you spend time wining and dining clients in great restaurants, or maybe your suppliers are keen to wine and dine you. Or perhaps you go to trade fairs in exotic locations. It's all very exciting for you, but these may not be things that your partner is able to take part in.

This is a potential source of resentment, but it is one that can be easy to address. If you discover a great restaurant in the company of a client, don't just tell your partner about it, go there the following week. If you fall in love with California during a trade mission, organize a holiday there at a later date. And if you stayed at a brilliant hotel, stay there again, this time with your partner. In other words, it's really important – if you can – to include your partner in all the good things that are happening to you.

But that probably won't happen if your life is tied entirely to a diary. You know how it is – every day is busy. From eight in the morning until nine at night, there are calls, meetings and networking events. Yes, you know that it's important to spend time with your partner just enjoying life, but you find yourself looking for gaps in a schedule. You find yourself saying, 'Why don't we book a restaurant. I'm available on Tuesday in three weeks' time.'

So, give yourself time to be spontaneous. If you find you are both available on a Tuesday, take the time to find something to do to rekindle that love.

Working from Home

One of the big attractions of running your own business is that you can – depending on what you do – work from home. That can be something of a joy. No more commuting into the city by train or getting stuck in traffic on a stretch of motorway. Instead, the journey from the breakfast table or shower to the office takes seconds. Following the pandemic, the smart money is on more and more people – and not just company owners – taking the work-from-home option.

But there are pros and cons. It can be isolating socially, and make things more difficult in terms of working relations with your team. More pertinently to this chapter, it can also be a source of tension with your partner.

Let's consider a couple of scenarios. Your partner comes home and finds a laptop and around thirty pages of notes spread across the kitchen table. Not a big problem perhaps, but it's been a long day and your business is 'kind of' getting in the way of them making a drink and relaxing free of clutter. It really is a good idea to establish – if possible – a space for work that doesn't impinge on the workings of the house.

Alternatively, you and your partner are entrepreneurs. You both work from home but on different projects. This creates a real danger that you will see too much of each other and that neither party has enough personal or working space. The way Bianca and I deal with this is to work in different rooms during the day and then join up in the same room later. It works for us.

There's probably a bigger question here about how much time you spend together and apart. Running a business can eat into a lot of personal time, so does that mean you spend the remaining hours catching up? And does that, in turn, suggest that you both spend less time with friends than you'd like?

Trigger Points

In this chapter, we've talked a lot about communication, but there are times when people find it difficult to talk about issues that are not only stressful but also potentially very damaging if they aren't addressed.

Consider this example. As an entrepreneur, you're running a new company on your own. You're making decisions each and every day that (as we discussed earlier) you might not be running past your partner at home. After a while, this becomes a mindset. You feel that you're the only one who understands the situation, so it's better not to share it with your partner. You don't even talk about the loss of a major client and the impact on income. It's something you're going to sort out yourself.

Meanwhile, your partner sees you coming back from work every day, looking increasingly stressed. Any attempt to ask you about the problem results in a brush-off reply and a look that says, 'Just leave me alone for the moment. I'm handling this.'

This isn't sustainable, not least because your shared welfare might be at stake. As a couple, you have to find a way of working around this. Maybe it's OK to keep things bottled up for a day or two, but if the problem doesn't go away or get sorted out by then it is essential to talk.

This goes a lot deeper than money or financial survival. You're bottling up stress and perhaps becoming more withdrawn. This has a detrimental effect on key elements – sex, intimacy, trust and communication – that hold relationships together.

Maybe your partner senses something is not right. Bianca will often say, 'Are you OK, babe? Do you want to talk about it?' That's a good start. It invites a conversation that you may or may not want to have at that moment. There are times when it's not a conversation I want to have and times when I do, the positive being that Bianca is OK with it being either and understands the difference between a talking day and a non-talking day. And when I am struggling she will typically make more of an effort with the things she knows I like, in an effort to be supportive.

If things are still difficult a week later, the question is repeated, and perhaps it's time to talk through the problem. If not, by week three or four, Bianca may give me little choice but to discuss it!

The secret is for both parties to understand each other well enough to know when it's the right time to hold back and when to press for more. This only works if a couple are prepared to be open with each other. Over time, habits such as secrecy and defensiveness become set in stone. As Professor Jennifer Petriglieri puts it: 'They become part of the culture of the relationship.'

Which takes us back to why communication is an essential tool and why it's vital to talk about the important issues at the point that going into business is first considered. This will create a culture of openness.

Sex and Intimacy

So, what happens when conversation breaks down? Put simply, it can mark the beginning of a long and probably troubled road that leads to the end of the relationship. In the meantime, it can also result in couples turning away from each other physically, as resentment and frustrations build.

If you're the sort of entrepreneur who works from home – either alone or with your partner present too – you might experience a falling off of desire at the best of times. Professor Petriglieri's research suggests that romantic partners are at their most attractive to each other when they are – temporarily – unattainable. For instance, you might be at a party having a conversation with someone. You look across the room, see your partner talking to friends and are overwhelmed with desire.

In contrast, the partner who is lolling around the kitchen in pyjamas and eating toast is probably not at their most attractive at that moment. This was observable at a big scale during the pandemic lockdown. Couples were shut up at home together and sex (according to the surveys) became less frequent.

Unresolved issues can put further strain on your sex life too. There is, however, some good news. 'A good sex life is often linked to things going well,' Petriglieri says. 'But the reverse can be true. When things are going badly, sex can help repair the damage.'

And the stresses of business life don't necessarily dampen the libido. Everyone is different in this respect. Some people shut themselves down when business problems arise, but others see their relationship and the associated intimacy as essential to staying balanced and grounded.

Ajiboye Dennis is a case in point. He is a driven entrepreneur, but his relationship with his fiancée helps keep the inevitable stresses of entrepreneurial life under control. 'To be honest, when I've had a stressful day, I want to have sex,' he says. 'I want to enjoy that moment – I want to make my partner happy and connect with her. It's about having that intimate moment and forgetting about all the fires I'm having to put out.'

Hence the importance of working at the romantic side of your relationship. Get out of the house. Go to parties, restaurants and the theatre. Take holidays together. If you need to schedule time, allocate date nights.

ENTREPRENEUR INSIGHT:
The 'Couplepreneurs'

Ajiboye 'Ryan' Dennis is the director of Quirky Hire, Photobooths London and the Photobooth Group UK. His fiancée, Malvia Morgan, is creative director of Quirky Hire. They have two children aged eight and thirteen. Today, they are both entrepreneurs working together in the Quirky Hire business, but that wasn't always the case. Balancing their family and romantic life with working commitments has been a long-standing challenge.

Ryan acknowledges that he has always found it hard to switch off. 'Being an entrepreneur is round the clock,' he says. 'You don't always know where your next meal is coming from.'

For Malvia, that was a double frustration. There were times when she just wanted Ryan to quit the entrepreneurial life and do something that offered financial stability. 'There have been times when I've said, "That's it, you have to get a job."' She knows Ryan is an entrepreneur through and through, 'but there has also been the challenge of finding time just to go for a walk or go for a meal. He will bring his laptop to lunch.'

Ryan is very analytical and knows his market well enough to know the peak times as well as the response time needed for his clients, but his five-minute-response rule has put pressure on their relationship.

Working together has made it easier for Malvia to understand the pressures of entrepreneurial life. Having formerly been the stable nine-to-five person in the relationship, she now feels like she is part of the greater vision for their family. Ryan, however, acknowledges that he could do more to make time for Malvia. The children are a priority, and between work and (for example) taking the eldest to football several nights a week, there is little time left for anything else. But there are solutions.

'I know I have to work on processes. I have more knowledge now that some of the things I've been doing could have been outsourced to other people,' Ryan says. This can be hard, however. Lowering his work intensity could result in things 'slipping away'. But, he says, the pandemic-enforced 'lockdown has helped me realize that you can outsource'.

Malvia agrees. 'He has always been an amazing parent and an amazing businessman. Being an amazing partner has been a work in progress, but since [the pandemic] lockdown, he gets that a lot more.'

Working together has also meant much more time together, which has been good. The next step? 'I need to add processes, and those processes will free up time – to have more romantic time together,' says Ryan.

Children and Family Life

Bianca and I don't have any children yet but, as any parent will tell you, the arrival of a child – possibly followed by at least one more – changes everything. You have less disposable income. You have to juggle a whole new set of roles and responsibilities.

As *Company of One* author Paul Jarvis points out, the arrival of a child can reset your business priorities. It may well be that the 'comfortable' income you considered sufficient is no longer enough. And this can create real pressure.

Let's go back to our 'one in, one out' scenario, with one partner working as an employee and the other running a business. Employment income could drop if the employee partner takes a cut in hours or leaves work completely. Now it's up to the business owner to make the difference. As Mark Dixon noted (see p. 170), it's enormously helpful if you have family who can help with childcare – but that won't be the case for everyone.

There's a lot to discuss. The financial contributions that will be required for children should be reviewed and any new costs – including childcare – need to be factored in.

Children are also an incentive to succeed. As Ajiboye 'Ryan' Dennis points out, the stakes are higher: 'Before I had children, if I had failed as an entrepreneur I could simply have gone back and stayed at my mum's. You can't do that when you have children. Their welfare has to be a priority.'

There's a deeply emotional element too. Many parents – and this is not unique to entrepreneurs – feel guilty about working too hard when their children are young. Perhaps that guilt isn't necessary. According to Jennifer Petriglieri's research, children don't resent the hard work of their parents. 'Actually, children see their parents and they learn about work,' she says. 'The work that their parents do is incredibly important to children. And one of the joys of being an entrepreneur is bringing children into your work.'

Nevertheless, parents benefit from the support of those around them. 'We need a village to raise kids,' she says. 'That's much better than if the kids grow up in a tiny nuclear family.'

Single and Searching

Much of what I've talked about so far has focused on relationships that have a degree of permanency – or, if relatively new, the potential to become something that survives and thrives beyond the first few dates. Thus, many of the problems and challenges discussed have essentially revolved around making an existing relationship work – and work well – when entrepreneurship represents the third point on the triangle.

But let's take a step back. Sometimes there isn't a triangle. There is just the entrepreneur and a new business and a question to be asked. And it goes something like this: 'Things are going well at the moment, but I know that for the next five or six years I'm going to have to put everything – heart and soul – into creating the company that I've always dreamed of. So do I have time for a relationship – and frankly, even if I do, would a romantic entanglement fit in with my plans?'

Let's be honest, there will be times when an entrepreneur might feel that they have to devote every waking minute to building their business. There is simply no time for a partner. If that's the case, it may not be the right moment to begin anything more than the most casual of relationships. Though time – or the perceived shortage of it – is an obstacle that can probably be addressed through a degree of negotiation.

A potentially thornier issue arises when someone is unsupportive – or even actively dismissive. Now, in reality, most people starting out in new relationships are subtler than that – unless they're looking for ways to end things there and then – but there usually are still indications. Certainly, many entrepreneurs detect warning flags during early conversations – signs that their new friend is unlikely to be supportive. And if your passion is to create something great, this can be a deal-breaker.

Similar scenarios occur further down the line when businesses are more established. At this point, the problem may be that new or prospective partners feel somehow threatened or sidelined by the commitment and sense of purpose of the entrepreneur. The tensions that emerge mean that the relationship won't – and probably wasn't meant to – thrive.

From research, it appears that many women have a particular problem finding partners who accept their commitment to entrepreneurship. It's a common complaint that men often feel threatened by the dynamism of women who run successful businesses. At the other end of the spectrum, men who are ambitious and dynamic can be competitive rather than supportive within a relationship. However, this isn't always a case of gender but rather one of male and female energies – I'm sure we all know of situations where the stereotypical roles have been reversed.

Male and Female Energies

Male and female energies are not directly related to biological sex. All of us, regardless of who we are, contain a mix of 'feminine' and 'masculine' qualities – otherwise known as yin and yang. Empathy, a strong awareness of thoughts and feelings, creativity, and a warrior spirit are often seen as feminine characteristics. Masculine characteristics might include a sense of adventure, action-orientation and protectiveness.

Now, everyone knows that there are plenty of men who are strongly aware of the feelings of others, and there are a huge number of women who are adventurous and action-oriented. In this respect, the assignment of yin and yang is best seen as a kind of road map that helps us look at the balance within our own personalities.

The problem arises when cultural stereotypes get in the way – when we expect women to act one way and men another. When women go into business, they are often seen as stepping into a masculine realm and doing it with gusto. And frankly, this freaks some men out.

So here's the problem. At one end of the scale, you have men who don't understand the vision for the business or who feel threatened or undermined by strong women. At the other end, you have highly competitive men who may get the vision but have no wish to be outshone by someone else's entrepreneurial energy. In fairness, the same problem can run in the other direction.

The upshot is that it can be hard for an entrepreneur to find someone. The gene pool of suitable partners is smaller.

So what's the answer to this conundrum? It may simply be that if you're looking for a long-term – or even medium-term – partner, it's important to consider your priorities and what you need in a significant other. This may mean being very selective.

ENTREPRENEUR INSIGHT:
Finding Love and Running a Business

*'I have made a conscious effort to apportion more time for dating,'
says Samantha Clarke, author of* Love It or Leave It *and founder
of the Growth and Happiness School. 'But it comes in waves,
depending on how my business is doing.*

*'In the past I've found it very easy to lean into my business. At
the same time, I haven't had the most successful relationships.
Compatibility and suitability have been issues. My sickle cell has
been an issue and not every man is strong enough to see the one he
loves in a lot of pain.*

*'A lot of men have been in awe of what I do – they tell me how
they looked me up on Google. That's not what I want. I want to be
just as interested in them as they are in me. There are men who are
very happy in nine-to-five jobs and who don't have passion and
purpose. Which, put simply, isn't interesting to me. On the other
side, there are men who are very driven and tenacious but overly
competitive. One said to me: "You can't have two people driving and
now I'm in the driver's seat."*

*'It's not always easy to meet suitable partners. Coaching is a very
female-dominated industry. But now I'm spending more time with
CEOs, people in finance and property. That's a much more male
environment.*

*'And now I have made space to have a relationship and I do have
a clear idea of what I want. Someone with a strength of mind and
a passion for business, but also someone who is fluid enough to have
a life in London and internationally – in the Caribbean or Africa. I
also want a kindred spirit who sees the opportunities to leave a
legacy.'*

A Supportive Perspective

Let's not forget, however, that being the partner of a successful person can require a significant degree of psychological adjustment – at least in certain circumstances.

I have personal experience of this. Bianca is not only extremely successful; she also enjoys a very high public profile thanks to her television appearances. That's something that I feel totally positive about. From my perspective, who wouldn't want to date and ultimately marry a boss – someone who aspires to achieve great things and is in charge of her own destiny.

But at times I have had to think about my role, at least regarding the public face of our relationship. I accompanied Bianca to a lot of events and people would come up and say, 'Hi, Bianca. So nice to see you again,' or words to that effect. Very often, my presence wouldn't be acknowledged.

That was a surprise. I'm six foot two and I have a presence, but people were acting as if I wasn't there, even though Bianca would make a point of introducing me.

At first, I thought this was very bad-mannered, but I came to realize that people weren't deliberately setting out to be rude; it was just the dynamic of the situation. At these events, Bianca was the focus of their attention – after all, she had received the invite – and I was just there to support her. I was the plus-one. That was the reality, but it did require me to look at things from a new perspective.

The converse can be true as well. There are times when Bianca attends an event – say an awards night at which I am featured – and she is treated in much the same way. It's not necessarily a man/woman thing. Nevertheless, men can find it tougher to deal with. As Bianca points out, if you book into a hotel or go to a restaurant as a couple, the chances are the check-in clerk or waiter will address the man first, assuming he will deal with the transaction.

So, from the perspective of a partner, how do you deal with this kind of situation? Well, it's not that difficult. You just accept that, on certain occasions, you are there to provide support. You are not there to be the centre of attention. But that doesn't necessarily mean you sit around like a wallflower. I see these events as an opportunity to network.

And there is a bigger picture to consider here. In a relationship – certainly in a good relationship – you should be supporting your partner in their ambitions. I am always trying to elevate Bianca, even to the extent of putting her success before mine if necessary.

The important thing is to feel secure in yourself. I am successful, and I make my own money. Therefore I have no trouble slipping into a supportive role. It is, after all, an amazing thing to be in a relationship where both partners are aspiring to do great things.

But a supportive role can be tough for those who haven't got their own act together and who consequently wrestle with insecurity. That's why it's important to be selective. Finding someone who will support you is an important part of choosing a partner.

A Relay, Not a Sprint

There really are no quick fixes for some of the problems that can arise within relationships in which one or both parties is an entrepreneur. And that's partly because we aren't talking about fixed moments in time. A good relationship can last a lifetime. Equally, anyone starting a business should be in it for the long haul. Within these extended time frames, a huge amount can happen.

So, let's be realistic. You might agree on the finances of your business within the context of the relationship today, only to find that circumstances change tomorrow. You might decide to have children. One partner could lose their job or a business, requiring the other to shoulder a bigger financial burden for a while. A few years later, the reverse could happen. Or the business that requires a sixteen-hour day could be almost running itself in ten years' time.

In other words, nothing stands still as circumstances change, and the role of each partner will also alter. You might be supporting your partner this year. Next year, it might be you that requires a degree of financial (and perhaps also emotional) support.

As Professor Jennifer Petriglieri points out, the balance of support and responsibility within a relationship will shift. 'Ideally, it should be a fifty-fifty thing,' she says. 'But the equity within a relationship will work itself out over time.'

Think in terms of a relay rather than a marathon; each partner will pass the baton to the other at points along the journey. It's also important to remember that the relay is a team race. One partner may be faster or be able to run further, but in order to win – to reach the finish line – both parties need to be in the game. That might be difficult for one partner to see if – at any given time – they feel they are carrying too much of the burden, but it is important to look to the bigger picture and the common vision.

One key to relationship longevity is trust and affection. 'Think kindly about the other person,' Professor Petriglieri advises. 'Kindness really matters.' Particularly during tough times.

In the final analysis, assuming you and your partner agree on the common vision, there is a huge amount to talk about. But at the heart of things, there are four simple questions:

- How can I support you?
- How can you support me?
- What will you do to support me?
- What will I do to support you?

And perhaps we could add a fifth question. Within a relationship, what is enough – and when is it enough, if you have set a deadline for the business – for both parties?

Chapter Nine

Deal with Rejection, Conflict and Failure

'Let us never negotiate out of fear.
But let us never fear to negotiate.'

– John F. Kennedy

You can't run a business without conducting negotiations and striking deals; it's part of the game. Whether it's getting a discount from a supplier, talking prices and delivery times with a potential customer, or hammering out the details of an agreement to buy a rival business, you'll probably never be too far away from a dealmaking situation.

And for a great many entrepreneurs, doing deals represents the very essence of being in business. To the committed dealmaker, successfully completing a deal is about more than banking the cash, it's also an act of self-affirmation.

Why? Well, because a completed deal is a manifestation of a combination of human attributes – including determination, market knowledge and negotiation skills. You could even say that the deal is an art form in itself. What's more, pulling off a big negotiation is pretty thrilling.

That's the upside. But what about those times when you hit setbacks? A potential customer says no, and that happens several times in succession. Another prospect proves hard to contact – no matter how many times you try. When the deals don't happen, it can be a challenge to remain motivated.

But stay motivated you must. For the truth is that dealing with rejection, setbacks and even conflict is one of the 'costs' of doing business or succeeding in the workplace.

So, if you're to succeed over the long term, it's important to do two things. First, you need to take steps to give yourself the best possible opportunity of striking a deal. And second, you need to learn how to bounce back from the inevitable setbacks.

Who Are Your Customers?

The word 'deal' covers a multitude of situations ranging from the sale of a business – which may happen only one, two or three times in a lifetime – to raising capital from a bank or equity investment. But in this chapter, we'll be looking specifically at selling products or services to customers – something you'll be doing, or attempting to do, day in, day out, as you run your business.

The vital first step is to identify potential customers.

Ask yourself: do you know who your customers are? The answer to that question may not be as simple as it sounds. For instance, let's say you've designed and manufactured a range of accessories. They're a little bit edgy and you've concluded that your target customer is a woman aged between eighteen and thirty. It's not an exact science – you may pull in some younger, older or male customers, but essentially you've defined your battleground.

Or have you? Your target of 'women aged between eighteen and thirty' is not a homogeneous group. Beneath that broad demographic umbrella, there are huge variations in terms of income, culture and taste. So, you need to know more about your audience. Where do they shop? What media do they consume? How does your product fit in with known consumption patterns and habits? Will enough people within your chosen demographic be willing to pay the asking price, or will they find it too expensive or not sufficiently unique to justify a premium price? Conversely, will the product be deemed 'too cheap' by key sections of the target audience?

You can only answer these questions by engaging with – and, thus, getting to know – your target customers. And that means you have to find them.

Exactly how you do this will depend on the type of business you run. Some businesses – a high street newsagent springs to mind – attract an enormously broad demographic, and finding customers can be as easy as renting a well-placed shop space in a busy area and waiting for people to come through the door. The majority of businesses, however, are aiming their products and services at specific customer groups. For instance, an IT solutions company targeting small- and medium-sized businesses in the local area; or a beauty products venture seeking space on the shelves of key retailers, while also selling online to women (or indeed men) within a clearly defined age group.

This is where things begin to get a bit more challenging. Let's take the example of the IT company that plans to sell to local firms. The target companies themselves are probably relatively easy to identify – a quick trawl through a local directory will provide a long list. But who do you speak to? Who handles procurement? And do they really need what you're selling?

Happily, there are a number of tried-and-trusted channels that you can use to engage with your prospects. In the business-to-business arena, these include networking events, referrals and social media platforms. LinkedIn, in particular, is a hugely effective way of finding the right people to speak to and then opening a dialogue.

Now let's look at each of these in detail.

The LinkedIn Effect

Established in 2002, LinkedIn currently has more than 700 million members. Perhaps more importantly, 260 million of them use the business-oriented social network at least once a month. According to LinkedIn itself, 90 million of its users are senior-level influencers.

In other words, LinkedIn members are numerous and well connected. But the real value of the platform lies in its mission to connect people who are seeking to expand their businesses and further their careers. Unlike, say, Twitter, Facebook or Instagram,

LinkedIn members tell you exactly who they are in terms of the company they work for, their job title, their responsibilities and (sometimes, at least) what they hope to achieve by being on the network. Helpfully, LinkedIn also encourages members to provide a comprehensive list of previous positions. As such, it's a gold mine of business intelligence, and a great source of leads.

LinkedIn is searchable by company. So if you want to know who does what with, say, Virgin Atlantic, you simply key in the company name, and all the people who work there (along with those who have worked there in the past) will be displayed on-screen. This makes it the ultimate 'search and destroy' tool. If you want to find the name of a procurement chief with a particular organization, the information you need is just a few keystrokes away.

And once you've done your search, you can engage – either by asking to connect or, if you're a premium member, messaging them using LinkedIn's internal email tool (InMail to its friends). Making a connection is the easiest option. Relatively few people turn down LinkedIn connection requests, as just about everyone on there has registered in order to expand their online networks. It is, however, quite passive. While the other user may have accepted your request, they probably don't really know who you are or what you want.

Sending a personal message is much more proactive. It can be quite simple. For instance, let's say you've read a LinkedIn article posted by someone you would like to talk to. An opening gambit via InMail might be: 'Hi Joanna – I read your article on business recovery after a crisis. I love what you and your team are doing. My company works in a complementary field. Would it be possible to talk on the telephone or via video call?'

If you use LinkedIn as a research tool, the chances are you'll be reaching out to prospective customers and/or partners regularly. That doesn't mean you have to write a new message each time. The most efficient thing to do is to create a number of message templates that can be stored in a Word or Google Docs file and cut and pasted into LinkedIn's messenger app when necessary. That will save a lot of time, but remember to personalize the message for each recipient.

Nothing reflects worse on you than a message that reads like (if we're being charitable) an advert or (to be brutally honest) spam.

This kind of messaging is a conversation. Your first communication should say something about why you are making contact, who you are, what you do and how you can add value. But it should also contain a call to action, a question designed to generate a response – i.e. don't simply end the message with 'I hope to hear from you' without a call to action like 'when would you be available to schedule a call?'

EXERCISE:
Create a LinkedIn Message Template

Put together a message template that is designed to open a conversation with a prospective customer. It should look something like this:

- An introduction, briefly setting out who you are and what you do.
- An explanation of what prompted you to make contact. For instance, maybe a mutual contact suggested you get in touch.
- Explain the purpose of the message. What is your specific reason for making contact with this person?
- A call to action. This should be something that prompts a reply. You could, for example, ask for more information about the recipient's company.

Here's an example:

Good afternoon [insert name]
    Thank you for connecting with me. I am a big believer in building stronger networks so I thought I ought to introduce myself – I am the founder of a personal branding consultancy called The Be Group.

We specialize in helping individuals understand the value of their personal brand on their career trajectory. We offer workshops/training to enhance and support the career trajectory of employees across the career life cycle. Our workshops are created to improve the personal brand, communication, leadership impact and networking skills of our delegates. We are known in the industry for our ability to provide engaging, interactive, actionable and thought-provoking sessions. We also offer personal brand mentoring for those who require individual support.

I am reaching out because we have worked with a number of organizations similar to yours (including the likes of Accenture, Google, Barclays, De Beers, Facebook, BlackRock, EY, PwC, CMS, HSBC, Schroders, etc.) and I thought we might be able to add great value for you.

Please let me know your availability for a call in the coming days, as it would be great to discuss your agenda for this year with you in more detail.

I look forward to hearing from you!

Regards

Bianca

You don't have to stay within LinkedIn, of course. Once you know who the best contacts are within an organization, it shouldn't be too difficult to find out their phone numbers and email addresses. Indeed, if they respond positively to an approach via LinkedIn, you'll probably be swapping phone numbers as a matter of course.

Having a range of communication options is useful. For one thing, not everyone uses LinkedIn regularly or enthusiastically. So, if a prospect doesn't respond via InMail, you may have better luck with email or phone.

Sowing Seeds

It's worth remembering that LinkedIn is also a means to proactively bring your business to the attention of potential customers, partners, employees and mentors. Your personal profile is a starting point, and it's important to provide a comprehensive overview of what you and your company do. This helps people to find you via search.

You can also write and post articles. These can help you establish a reputation as an expert in your field or a thought leader. Again, this makes it more likely that people will seek you out. Or, when you make contact with others, they might well already know who you are.

Networking and Referrals

The same profile-raising principle can be applied to networking events. As you make contacts and strike up conversations, you will increase the number of people who know who you are and what you offer ahead of any formal business approach.

We've already looked in detail at the art of networking, but it's worth saying in this context that word of mouth (online and offline) is still one of the most effective methods of identifying potential customers or partners. At a networking event, you may talk to people who are in the market for the service you offer. Equally, however, you are almost certain to know people who will point you in the right direction and perhaps even recommend you to someone they know.

You can certainly use both your own network and networking events to secure referrals, but this needs to be done with care. Think of it this way – you are anxious to speak to the chief procurement officer of a mid-sized company, and you find out that someone in your own circle has a personal connection. That person might be a mentor, a friend of a friend, or a relative. All of which sounds nicely tight-knit and cosy. So why not ask for a helping hand in the form of an introduction?

Well, because you might be asking a favour too far. Remember, your mentor – to take one of the examples – has their own relationship with this particular procurement officer. It's a relationship that shouldn't be compromised. Thus, you should only ask for an introduction or referral if you're absolutely sure that your business can genuinely add value.

Byron and I have personal experience of this. A mentee might ask for an introduction. Now, we want to provide as much support as possible, but we won't refer or recommend anyone unless we're sure that a meeting would be beneficial to both parties. If there isn't clarity about the value you offer, any request for a referral is likely to be turned down. And it probably should be.

All your relationships should be mutually beneficial. It is bad practice to seek to exploit a relationship with a member of your network without good reason. To put it bluntly, you should avoid any perception that you are a parasite.

The Approach – Solving a Problem

What do we mean by 'adding value'? It is, admittedly, something of an abstract term. Well, as you prepare to approach a prospective customer or client, it's helpful to think of your offer in terms of the problem that it solves. For instance, during the Covid-19 pandemic, a great many businesses found themselves managing staff who were working from home. This created a whole new way of working. Suddenly, businesses that had never used messaging, video-conferencing or collaboration tools found they had to do so. Others had already deployed those tools previously, but now had to extend the use of them to a larger number of people.

So here was a clear example of a problem that required a

solution. So much so that suppliers of collaboration software were among the select group of businesses to benefit directly from the crisis.

But even in that situation, an approach to a customer could not be regarded in any way as a 'shoo-in'. Even at a time when a huge percentage of the population was working from home, no one could assume that any one company required a particular solution.

The truth is that before you pitch a proposal to a prospective customer, you need to spend time building a relationship with them and gathering information.

Researching the Customer

As you engage with a prospect, you should be asking yourself a sequence of questions:

- What problem is the prospect facing?
- What, if any, is the current solution?
- What is the individual or company looking for at this time?
- Who can you help?

Once you have an overview of the prospect's situation via your research, the next step is to engage in a fact-finding exercise.

Which brings us back to those channels of engagement we were talking about. Whether you use LinkedIn or identify a client through a network or a recommendation, at some stage you will move from making contact – getting on the radar – to having a conversation. This could take place in person, on the phone or even by an exchange of email. But once the conversation begins, your primary job is to get to know your prospect.

EXERCISE:
Customer Fact Finding

Sit down with a piece of paper and write down twenty-five questions that – typically – you might use to move a conversation with a prospect forward.

The questions should be designed to uncover any problems that your client faces, and how your business can address those issues. But you should also be digging deeper and finding out as much as you can. For instance:

- You know there's a problem, but how important is it?
- Can the prospective client articulate the problem?
- What have they tried before?
- Who have they used?
- What was wrong with the previous option/supplier that they tried?
- What kind of budget is available? Will this be a sophisticated, premium solution, or something off the shelf?
- More widely, what are the company's values, priorities and timelines? How soon would they like to start?
- What does the ideal solution look like for them?

Once you know what your client is looking for, you will be in a much better position to pitch a proposition, because you'll have all the information.

There is rarely any such thing as a cookie-cutter proposal. No two sets of requirements will be entirely the same. And whether you're pitching to an individual or a team, personalities will to a greater or lesser extent affect the dynamic of your discussions. So try to understand how your customers think and see the world.

To Negotiate or Not

Some prospects will be prepared to negotiate. Others would rather simply say no than enter into a situation that may involve a degree of give and take. Even in the business world, there can be a reluctance to discuss money or haggle over a deal. Nevertheless, you should be prepared to negotiate, if and when it is required.

This can be a daunting prospect, not least because negotiation involves making decisions about what is and isn't acceptable. You may approach a prospect with the intention of selling a product at a unit price of £5.00. The potential customer's response is to say, 'Could you go down to £4.20?' which is a figure that you hadn't considered. Is your prospect bluffing? Would trying to push the price back up to a more acceptable £4.60 be a deal-breaker? And would you want to do a deal at that level anyway? If you accepted £4.20, would you feel slightly cheated?

Meanwhile, the prospect will also be doing a lot of mental calculations of their own.

You can help yourself in this situation by:

- Understanding the prospect's requirements.
- Being absolutely clear – in advance – about what you need in terms of margin.

If possible, ask your client about their budget. Knowing, roughly, what the customer is prepared to spend will help you formulate a price. Now, the client won't necessarily tell you up front. Indeed, making a supplier quote a price blind can be a negotiating tool. The psychology behind this is that the seller will attempt to win the business by going low.

But what you certainly can do is research the market. If you know, roughly speaking, what competitors are charging for similar products or services, you'll be in a strong position to put together a proposal and a price that will be in line with the market norm.

Through your preliminary discussions – when you asked questions and listened to the answers – you should also have got a sense of the prospect's goals. Why is your product required? What will it help the buyer to achieve? How much do they really need it? And can they easily go elsewhere? Who is their current supplier? Again, this kind of knowledge provides leverage in the negotiation.

Using Silence

Negotiation is not only an art form but also a little bit of psychological trickery, and skilled negotiators use psychology to achieve their objectives. But you can also deploy some of the tricks of the trade. In our negotiations, Byron and I have found that silence can be a powerful weapon. Silence makes people nervous and leaves them feeling slightly unsure of their position. This sense of uncertainty can break a negotiation stalemate.

Let's carry on that example from above. The prospect sticks to the position that a unit cost of £4.20 is fair. You know that's too low. You also know from your research that the prospect really needs the product you're offering, and that £5.00 is actually a great unit price.

Stay quiet. Let the seconds tick away as the tension grows. Maybe then your client will move towards a more acceptable price point. It's often said that the person who breaks the silence first loses.

Getting Creative with a Win-Win

But what if there's an impasse? What if there's no apparent way of bridging the gap between the price you need to achieve and the cost that the prospect feels is justified? Or, in a slightly different scenario, what if both parties have talked themselves into a corner and feel they can't move without losing face?

Then it's time to be creative. You can begin to move beyond price and discuss other factors that could make the deal happen.

If you've ever bought a house, you'll know how this can work. A seller puts the property on the market at £450,000 and – buoyed by optimistic noises from an estate agent – that price is seen as rock solid. Anything below that level is a deal-breaker.

Meanwhile, the buyer has a budget of £420,000 and that figure also appears to be set in stone. So what other factors can be brought into play to move things forward? Well, if the seller agrees not to accept any subsequent offers from other parties, that might encourage the buyer to raise their offer because it reduces risk. If the buyer can provide assurances that there is no chain involved – that buying this house is not dependent on selling another – the seller may agree to bring the price down to accelerate a sale. Or the intermediary might be persuaded – in view of market conditions – to suggest that the seller lowers the price. Ultimately, a deal is struck.

Similarly, in business, creative solutions can make a difference. If as a seller you accept a lower price, the quid pro quo might be an agreement that the buyer will honour all invoices within fourteen days – providing a cash flow boost, even if the unit cost is lower.

Underpromise, Overdeliver

OK, so the deal is done. Time to pop the champagne and celebrate. Well, perhaps, but the work isn't over. You still have to deliver. That gives you an opportunity not just to meet expectations but to exceed them.

The trick is to deliver more than you promise. This will create goodwill and make repeat orders more likely. But what does that look like in practice?

Here's an example. Byron runs a 'pick my brains Friday' session for prospective clients/mentees. It's fifteen minutes in which six people can ask questions. But although it's scheduled for fifteen minutes, he always has the flexibility to run over by five minutes. The extra time is factored in to Byron's timetable, but participants in the session see it as a bonus. From their perspective, it demon-strates that Byron is willing to do something extra.

There are all sorts of things you can do that add value. If you run a consultancy – like Byron – don't stress if the sessions run over their allotted time at the end of the day, and try to address every-one's questions, within limits. If you're selling a tangible product, maybe you can deliver earlier than promised if that will help the customer. Always have something in your locker that will sweeten the deal without costing you too much.

Feedback

They say 'feedback is a gift', and everyone likes to get good feed-back from their customers. If someone tells you the service you're providing is excellent, that's a great feeling. And better still, you might be able to turn that into the kind of testimonial that will help you to win more work.

On the flip side, no one likes negative feedback. Ironically, though, it can be the most useful kind of response. Assume for a moment that you're dealing with two customers who have been largely silent. You assume they're happy. Then a third provides some negative feed-back. That's clearly not good, but if the comments are fair and actionable you can use them to improve your service for everyone and address issues that you might otherwise have been unaware of.

Public feedback can be more problematic. These days, you might find reviews posted on your own website, on social media or on a third-party site such as Amazon or Tripadvisor. The principle of learning from your mistakes and putting things right still applies, but you might also need to do some rapid public relations / damage limitation work. That could involve contacting the negative reviewer to apologize and offer compensation or assurances that the service will improve. Or you might respond publicly, putting forward your own side of the story. Critics are not always right – and sometimes complaints are unjustified.

When the Customer Says No

And that brings us rather neatly to the difficult side of dealmaking – those times when the negatives begin to pile up. Sometimes the customer says yes and all goes well. Sometimes you get some negative feedback, but you deal with it.

But whatever business you're in, you're going to have to deal with occasions – and they are likely to be the majority – when you fail to make a sale. Or some other type of deal falls through. Some rejections are easy to shake off. If you're selling cold and you make ten calls in a morning, the negative impact of eight rejections is likely to be counterbalanced by the two calls that generate a positive result. But what if you're making calls – or trying to book meetings for a month or more – without any sign of a positive response? What happens when you pursue a big order through a lengthy tendering process and fall at the final hurdle? It can seem like hitting a wall. The first really huge order might be next week, but you don't know that. The truth is, a succession of rejections can eat away at your confidence – as can the loss of a single but really important contract.

But you must learn to deal with it. We all encounter problems. They can be frustrating or deep-seated, but they must not be allowed to dominate us or define our sense of who we are and what we are capable of achieving.

In business, work or life, we all need to build resilience. Sometimes that resilience is inherently part of an individual's personality, manifesting as clear, unstoppable determination. But through reflection and analysis we can also nurture the kind of strength that will enable us to overcome obstacles.

Accepting Your Own Reality

There are ways in which we can undermine ourselves – even before the first prospective customer has uttered the first 'no'.

Human beings are not homogeneous. We all come from different ethnic, cultural and educational backgrounds. When the time comes to start a business, we might do so at the age of eighteen, eighty or anywhere in between.

At certain times in our life, we might feel that we are being held back by our age. We're too young. Or we're too old. In a male-dominated profession, maybe it seems like being a woman is a handicap. Or we may feel hampered by a whole cocktail of attributes – not only age and gender, but perhaps also our ethnicity.

When I started The Be Group and went to my first few meetings, I had a feeling that some people were visibly surprised when they saw me. That might have been because of my age (I was twenty-two) or possibly because of my race. I felt that people were looking at me as if to say, 'Oh, you're Bianca!' – and some even said as much. It seemed like they were expecting someone else to be sitting on the other side of the table.

And it didn't feel positive. My business is personal branding within organizations. Through my eyes, it looked as if they were making a judgement, or at least asking a question: 'Who is this young woman who feels she can come in here and tell us what to do?'

So I spoke to my dad and he said simply: 'You're young, you're black, you're female – that is your reality. What are you going to do about it?'

What I did was go into meetings and take control of the situation. I got clients to focus on the value I could bring by highlighting my knowledge and skill set, thus providing the assurance that I could do what I said I could do – and more.

Reframing Challenge as Opportunity

There are, of course, realities other than those springing from who we are as individuals. At times we are all faced with circumstances that could be considered adverse or indeed very difficult indeed. Witness the Covid-19 pandemic. Scientists had been predicting an outbreak of this type for years, but when the crisis hit, it was – for most people – out of the blue and potentially devastating. Some businesses faced problems with supply. Others with demand. And in many cases, both were affected.

During the crisis, I had lots of clients postpone or cancel events suddenly – some without any clarity on a new date. One client moved the date and then reached out to say they would have to cancel – in truth the notice period meant they would still have to pay, but that wasn't the focus for me. The focus was on overcoming the obstacle. How could I better the situation for my client and their delegates? And how could I also develop myself in the process?

I had been well and truly battered that week by cancellation emails, and I could easily have found myself a dark, quiet corner. Instead, I emailed them and said: 'Let's talk about bringing it online.' We had a call, and they asked if I had done it before. The truth was yes, I had for other clients, but they had managed the tech. Had I done it at home on my laptop? No, absolutely not.

So I took my cue from Richard Branson, who once said: 'Say yes – then learn how to do it later!' I consulted the tech, and I learned how to use Zoom very quickly! Then I delivered successfully to twenty delegates (plus five senior staff from my client's company who wanted to see what the session was like online). And you know what that did – it made me their saviour for that event, and it showed them I could deliver content online.

In situations like this, clearly you can't carry on as normal. But what you can do is find alternative (and perhaps also creative) ways of working. You can take control. Every crisis or upset is different, but when dealing with adversity you should look for ways to reframe the challenge as an opportunity.

You Are Not Alone

During challenging times, it's important to remember that you are not alone – or you shouldn't be. During the pandemic, just about everyone faced struggles. There were times when it was difficult to buy fresh food. Many employees found themselves working from home for the first time, perhaps surrounded by children and partners. Business owners wrestled with a range of good, less good and bad options, as they put plans in place to stay afloat. But this was not happening to individuals in isolation. And all over the country, people were coming up with ideas and solutions.

There are usually opportunities to reach out to people who can help you. These might be friends, family, other business owners or people in your business network. Many of you who are reading this book today will have sought out (or be seeking) mentors or coaches. A crisis – such as the Covid-19 pandemic – is a time when mentors can come into their own, providing not just advice but genuine psychological support. Certainly, Byron and I ensured that we made ourselves available to our mentees.

Flowing around the Obstacle

As movie star Sylvester Stallone once said, 'I take rejection as someone blowing a bugle in my ear to wake me up and get going, rather than retreat.' Thankfully, pandemics and even major recessions are relatively rare occurrences. The obstacle you are likely to encounter most often is the word 'no'.

But a 'no' can often appear to be more than just a bump in the road. For instance, winning a major client could be a key milestone in the development of your business. So what happens if, after weeks or perhaps months of positioning and negotiation, you fail to win the contract?

This shouldn't be seen as a disaster. Your job now is to surmount that obstacle, but before you do that, you need to establish a few facts.

Firstly, you really need to know why the potential customer turned you down. Or, to put it another way, what were the factors that caused your prospect to say no?

Sometimes you'll be told up front, but not always. While one potential customer may be brave or honest enough to say, 'Frankly, we didn't have the budget,' another might be reluctant to admit that cash was an issue. Similarly, your prospect might be bold enough to tell you openly that your product was inferior to the competition's. On the other hand, they could well fudge the issue for fear of seeming rude.

Whatever the initial response, you need to unpick the problem piece by piece until you uncover the root cause of your failure to win a sale. And this feedback may offer some light at the end of the tunnel. No may mean no (it often does), but if you press the point it may become apparent that the answer might be 'yes' when next year's budgets come on stream. And even if there won't be a second chance, an understanding of today's failure will help you hone your offer when you pitch to other customers in the future.

The question is, of course, what do you do with the information? If, for example, a prospect says you have a great product but it's too expensive, and what they require is something a little less good and considerably less expensive, how do you respond?

It's important to listen to feedback, and it's great if you can address some of the factors that may have been deal-breakers. But that doesn't mean you should rip up your business plan or ditch your product as it currently stands. Remember, you've done your research. You have a vision. And while making yourself aware of any factors that could stand between you and success, you should also be prepared to be persistent and determined in your pursuit of that vision.

That might require tweaks – or even a radical overhaul – of your offering, but that's not the same as setting the map for an entirely new destination. Always keep in mind your long-term plan, and take short- or medium-term actions to ensure that you ultimately get to where you want to be. As rapper Fabolous says in his song 'Gone for the Winter': 'My plan B's another way to make my plan A work.'

Making Plan B into Plan A

So how do you bounce back when you've apparently hit a brick wall? Well, if you're reading this book, you may also have read our first book, *Self Made*. As mentioned in the introduction, the route to publication was an exercise in overcoming rejection and moving forward towards success.

Our plan A was a book deal with a prestigious publisher, and when that didn't look like it would happen we realized that ultimately the plan was to get the book out there – so our Plan B was to do it ourselves. But, as the story goes, we did get a publishing deal after all and the book became a bestseller. The point being that it would have been easy to say: 'This isn't going to work, let's forget the whole thing, let's try something else.' But we didn't. We proactively pressed ahead and achieved our objective.

The bigger point here is that a 'no' can and should prompt you to think about alternative ways and means to make your vision a reality. If one approach doesn't work, try another. If you can't reach a prospect by phone, try email. If that doesn't work, go via LinkedIn or try to grab a conversation at a networking event. There are always options.

Staying in Touch

The relationship with a prospect doesn't necessarily end when you fail to win an order or contract. Indeed, it shouldn't. You've spent time nurturing the relationship. What's more, you've taken the trouble to ask why the deal didn't go through. It's more than likely there will be chances to pitch to them again in the months and years ahead.

So, just as you would with a paying client, stay in touch. Send a card at Christmas – remembering that writing the message yourself is more impressive than simply printing it out – and you can even take up LinkedIn's prompt to send a birthday message. This kind of ongoing engagement means your prospect will remember you – and favourably.

When appropriate, you can also call from time to time – again using the formula of asking questions and identifying problems.

Building Resilience

As Robin Black has pointed out: 'Rejection is part of the game. Or rather, rejection is part of the profession. A profession which at times can feel like a game.' Now, all of the above is very practical, but being on the receiving end of a 'no' has a psychological impact. As any athlete can tell you, there are times when you hit a winning streak, and you start feeling as if you can't lose. The confidence you're accruing actually spurs you on to play better. It's a virtuous circle.

The shadow of that is a downward spiral. Through no fault of your own, you hit a rough patch where nothing is working out and you begin to lose confidence. After a while, losing becomes the norm. You expect it, and your game suffers.

Clearly, that's not a helpful place to be. And it's not where you should be. Even in adversity – or in the middle of the kind of fallow period that occasionally befalls businesses – you need to maintain a positive mindset.

One way to look at rejection is to see it as nothing more than a change in direction on your way to achieving your goals. You adapt. You work around it. But it doesn't stop you.

Silencing Your Inner Critic

In the meantime, you'll undoubtedly have to cope with a jumble of emotions that could include disappointment, frustration and discouragement. Acknowledge those feelings. Don't pretend to yourself – or others – that everything is fine. After all, it probably isn't fine – you've just lost a major order. But by acknowledging those feelings, you can begin to use them as fuel to drive you forward.

Acknowledging your emotions is not the same as wallowing in them or allowing them to influence your sense of who you are and what you're capable of achieving. So it's important to ignore your inner critic – that voice in your head that says you were wrong to try. When your critic says, 'You know what, you were a bit stupid going after that deal,' cast that thought aside. Actually, you were brave and tenacious.

Nor should you allow your critic to tell you that failure defines you. It doesn't. Failure happens. Everyone loses a sale. Everyone fails to finalize a deal. But today's failure is just a point in time. It doesn't tell you anything about future outcomes. It doesn't mean you won't strike a similar deal tomorrow or the day after. In fact, what failure can certainly do is provide knowledge that will help you to do better next time.

Resilience through Activity

Focused activity builds resilience. The best response to a failure, big or small, is to go at the problem again from another angle. I have been in scenarios where one person at a firm says no and another says yes. It's important to take what you have learned and look at how you can reposition what you have to offer. Or try it again with another client in a similar industry – no loss there, just learning.

Equally, sometimes you'll find yourself playing a numbers game, and in order to win, you'll have to put in the hours. Remember the Pareto (or 80/20) principle – that 80 per cent of outcomes come from 20 per cent of causes?

One way to interpret that principle is to think about the number of calls you have to make to get a sale. Let's say you ring 100 numbers and only 20 bear fruit. Actually, that's not a bad ratio, but here's what you have to remember. You don't know which of those 100 prospects will buy what you have to sell. To succeed, you have to make all 100 calls. Realizing that will help you build your resilience.

When things aren't going well, it's worth asking yourself if you're doing enough. In his book *The 10× Rule*, Grant Cardone says individuals should set goals for themselves that are ten times greater than what they think they can achieve. To achieve those goals will require ten times more action – he calls it 'massive action' – than you think is necessary. Grant got it right: action drives success. So maybe – just maybe – if you've just binged your way through a few series of something on Netflix, you might consider how that time could have been used in pursuit of your goals.

Cardone also advises that, within your marketplace, you need to have the goal of becoming omnipresent. So ask yourself this: if people haven't heard of you, why not? And if they have heard of you, what are they hearing? Apply your energy to building a strong, credible and accurate presence.

The Power of No

So far we've talked mainly about how to maximize the chances of a 'yes' and how to deal with a 'no'.

But what about those times when we have to answer in the negative ourselves? As you become more successful, you'll find you get a lot of requests to do things that may or may not be useful to you. You'll be asked to speak at events, take part in panels, appear on local radio, or become a school governor or a non-executive director. Many of these things – arguably all of them – are thoroughly worthwhile, but you may not have the time. And on some occasions, you may be asked to do something for free that you would normally charge for.

Now, pro bono work is a good thing. Byron and I believe that it is very important to give something back. However, you do need to take a view on how much unpaid work you do. You can't do everything – there simply aren't enough hours.

Equally, when you're starting out, you may be asked to supply the first batch of a product at a discount, or agree to be paid within three months rather than one. It might be the right thing to do, but if it isn't then you quickly have to learn to say no.

The ability to answer in the negative can reinforce the value of what you do. Saying no is very powerful. However, remember to do so gracefully.

So what does that mean in practice? Well, Byron often deals with requests for my time. He's compiled a list of examples of how to turn down a request firmly without offending:

- *I'm sorry, but this event doesn't align with our current agenda.*
- *We can't say yes on this occasion, but we would be willing to reopen this conversation at a later date.*
- *Are you aware that this is what Bianca does to pay her bills? This is not something that we could consider doing without payment.*
- *As this doesn't align with your current budget, do you have any suggestions as to how we could take this forward?*
- *We have a pro bono quota and we've already reached that quota for this year.*
- *I can't see the benefit of doing that at this stage. Is there any further value you could add?*
- *No.*

Getting off a Sinking Ship

To succeed in business, you have to have faith in yourself and your vision. But that faith shouldn't be blind. The steps set out in this chapter provide a route map to understanding a prospective customer, making a proposition, maximizing the chances of securing a deal and moving on from any failures.

There may be times, however, when you have to accept defeat. That might mean closing a business completely, or calling time on a project or product that hasn't worked.

Business failure is a common occurrence. According to Britain's Office for National Statistics, around 60 per cent of new small businesses fail within five years. But that doesn't mean that the business owners fail. Many start new companies and succeed. The failure of a venture means only this: the project has not worked. That doesn't mean that your next business won't be a roaring success – assuming you learn the lessons.

But the really tough thing is making the decision and perhaps also living with consequences that go far beyond your own life. On a personal level, pulling down the shutters will feel like a major failure, but the decision will also affect staff, customers and suppliers. That represents a huge responsibility.

So, you may tell yourself that now is not the time. Another few weeks and the company's fortunes will be turned around. There is, after all, client interest. The big order is just around the corner. All that may be true. But you could also find yourself asking: does the hope of a turnaround justify throwing good money after bad?

It's a psychological rabbit warren. But, like a boxer, if you don't throw in the towel when the odds are firmly against you, you risk being knocked out.

So how do you decide? Well, as Byron points out, one crucial question revolves around your plan to effect a turnaround: 'You should ask yourself, "What can I do differently? What can I do to make this sustainable?"'

There's also a case for rating the benefits and costs of closing. On the benefits side, closure could mean peace of mind. A chance to draw breath, sleep, shake off months of stress and plan for the future. There could be a real sense of freedom. Against that there is the ripple effect of the business closing and the personal sense of loss. Why not list ten reasons to stay open and ten to close. If one list outweighs the other, this may give you an idea of whether it makes sense to stay trading.

No one wants to fail. No one wants to face rejection. But sometimes it happens, despite everyone's best efforts. The important thing to remember is that, assuming lessons are learned, failure can be a springboard to success.

Chapter Ten

Enjoy Your Success

'Success is a journey, not a destination.
The doing is often more important than the outcome.'

– Arthur Ashe

'I want success.' This is something Bianca and I hear all the time when we speak to people who are setting out on their own entrepreneurial journey. Perhaps it reflects a natural desire to encapsulate ambition in a few simple words.

Natural, maybe, but actually pretty unhelpful. The truth is you never really get 'success'. There is no single point along the road where you stop what you're doing, down tools and say, 'That's it. Job done. I've made it.'

That's not to say you shouldn't have clearly defined goals – you absolutely should. But the attainment of a particular goal is never really an endpoint. Rather, it is a milestone on a much bigger journey. There is always more to do, more to achieve and – crucially – more to enjoy.

And yes, it's important that you enjoy and appreciate what you do. That's not to say that every step along the entrepreneurial road will be free of stress and anxiety. There will always be obstacles to overcome, and there will also always be failures. But when you step back to look at the bigger picture, as an entrepreneur you are in an incredibly privileged position. Regardless of where your vision leads, you are someone who is shaping the world. You are putting your own ideas into practice and creating a life around them. This is something that you should relish.

Entrepreneurs – and indeed, ambitious people generally – rarely rest on their laurels. Richard Branson could probably have retired fairly comfortably on the proceeds from his record retail business. Instead, he went on to found airlines, a train company and dozens of other businesses – some successful, some not. In the process, he proved a master of brand extension.

Not everyone is quite so omnipresent as Branson, but even someone who starts and runs a single business across the course of their lifetime is rarely going to stand still. Over time, the business will change and evolve. New customers will come on board. Improvements will be made. Fresh opportunities will arise. Again, there is no single point of success.

In other words, the concept of simply wanting 'success' is something that you should set aside in favour of something deeper, richer and more fulfilling.

Bianca and I were once in a meeting with Aloki Batra, the CEO of the Five hotel group in Dubai, and he said: 'In business, sometimes you don't do something for the money, you do it because it is the right thing to do.' Surely that is the type of success we all seek.

Enjoying Success and Living for the Moment

But that perhaps begs a question. If there is no ultimate destination, if there is no point where the train stops, how do you stay motivated?

The answer – as we've alluded to – is simple. You take time out to enjoy the game you're playing.

Admittedly, that can be easier said than done. Consider a typical day. You might be putting out small fires, negotiating a major deal or simply hitting the phone from dawn to dusk. Meanwhile, members of your team are constantly in and out of your office with queries. There isn't much time to sit down with a coffee and reflect on what you've achieved or how much you enjoy doing what you do.

But you should. As entrepreneurs, we are probably all guilty of living too much in the future (making plans) or dwelling on the past (possibly not a good idea unless you're doing something constructive, like learning from your mistakes). What we don't often do is live in the moment. We don't take the time simply to think, 'Yes, there's a lot still to do – tomorrow, next week, next month and next year – but right here and right now I'm enjoying this experience.'

It's perhaps not mindfulness, but it's not a million miles away.

It's equally important to have fun. Everybody's business journey is different. In some – perhaps the majority – of cases, there will be months or years when money is tight and you have to budget carefully and focus all your efforts on work, learning tough lessons along the way. So it's even more crucial to take time to enjoy the fruits of your success. As things improve, enjoy the money you've made. Do the things you like doing. That's part of the reward.

The fun shouldn't necessarily be confined to the hours you spend away from the office, either. Like riding on a rollercoaster or whitewater rafting down a river, life in business can be scary – but that's what creates the adrenalin rush. There's a powerful sense of overcoming the odds. And that energy is what drives most successful people to carry on doing what they do.

The Law of Attraction

There are other energies you can tap into as well – not least your own creativity and ability to turn concepts, which may initially be only the germs of ideas, into reality.

Every action begins with a thought, whether it's making a cup of coffee or taking the first step down a road that could lead to the creation of a multimillion-pound business. That seems like an obvious statement, but our ability to think about and visualize our goals is an enormously powerful tool.

On one level, it's simple. You wake up in the morning and decide you want that cup of coffee, so you make one. Things get more interesting when you apply a slightly different principle. By focusing on your goals, visualizing them and embracing them as part of your life, you take one step (arguably several) towards turning your dreams into reality. Or to put it another way, you adopt a mindset that begins to attract the success you are looking for.

We all see 'attraction' in our day-to-day lives. For instance, have you ever noticed how like-minded people seem to be drawn to each other's company? We're not even talking, necessarily, about people who share an interest or a world view. It's something more fundamental than that.

Look around your extended friendship circle or the people you encounter in the workplace and you'll see something interesting. When it comes to forming deep relationships or even temporary alliances in support of a common goal, those with similar personality traits tend to band together.

Positive people will tend to team up with those who also display a can-do attitude. Of course, the same is true at the other end of the spectrum. People with problems tend to attract others who are also facing emotional or career difficulties. And those who tend towards negativity are often seen in each other's company.

It's complicated. This kind of attraction doesn't necessarily correlate with traits such as extroversion or intellect, or indeed any of the five big personality indicators defined by psychologists. For example, a two-person team of company founders comprising an extrovert and an introvert might well make a formidable combination, because each will bring different but complementary attributes to the table. But there is a common thread holding their alliance together too – namely a commitment to getting the job done.

There is something of a mystery here. As individuals, we don't always advertise who we are up front. And yet, again and again, like-minded people seem to find each other and establish bonds – often very rapidly.

And there is something else going on here as well. A positive outlook on life seems to correlate not only with some degree of success – and that will mean different things to different people – but also something that might lazily be described as 'good fortune'.

Likewise, negativity can often seem to generate a kind of feedback loop – and one that most of us have probably experienced at one time or another. Let's say you have a couple of bad experiences over a short period of time. Due to no fault of your own, you lose a couple of clients in a matter of weeks. That naturally affects your confidence, and it affects the way you run your business – perhaps driving a couple more bad decisions. All of a sudden, it seems as if you're attracting bad luck. (Hopefully, if your underlying confidence and optimistic outlook remain intact, you get yourself and your business back on track quickly.)

There is a relationship between our state of mind at any given time and the outcomes we achieve. Or, to put it another way, what we project to the world is reflected in what we attract. That might manifest in terms of friends or partners who arrive in our lives. Equally, our state of mind – what we project – can play a key role in attracting success.

What I've described thus far is a basic principle of attraction that can be witnessed just about anywhere. You could characterize it by the phrase 'You attract what you are'. All well and good, you might think, but it does seem a little random – not something that you can necessarily apply to your life in a conscious or systematic way.

Except you can.

A Step into Exciting Territory

Let's take a big step into unfamiliar but very exciting territory. As we've seen, everything we achieve in life begins with a thought. Today's thought is tomorrow's physical reality. Few people would argue with that statement.

But I promised you unfamiliar territory. Well, how about this. On one level, thought is nothing more than a necessary precursor to action, in a simple and easy-to-chart sequence of causes and effects that lead to an outcome. To hammer a nail into a wall, you must first make the decision to do so.

But thoughts also shape the material universe in a more fundamental way. Just as happy and optimistic people are drawn to each other, and just as those same character traits tend to correlate with success, people who approach life in a positive frame of mind, set themselves clear goals and expect that their ambitions will be fulfilled, often find that everything – or almost everything – they have expressly desired falls into their hands.

This is known as the 'law of attraction'. It works, and it has been working for thousands of years.

The Law and What It Means

You may already have heard about the law of attraction via Rhonda Byrne's *The Secret*, the definitive book on the subject and a worldwide bestseller. You may know that some of the world's most successful individuals, including Jim Carrey and Lady Gaga, have cited the principle of attraction as an important factor in their own success. But what exactly is it?

Put simply, the law of attraction states that each and every one of us has the capacity to attract what we want into our lives, initially by deciding on prioritized goals, asking a higher power – let's call it the universe – for help, and then visualizing those goals so intensely and vividly that they become part of our mental landscape, part of our sense of what and who we are.

At that point, the law of attraction takes over. The things we desire begin to spin into our orbit. What might once have seemed impossible or difficult to obtain becomes a tangible reality.

There is a caveat. It's not quite as simple as thinking about, say, a new car and expecting it to show up in the driveway a few days later. To successfully utilize the law of attraction, an individual will typically have to deploy a range of disciplined mental techniques – including the aforementioned visualization – in concert with the kind of hard work that all of us need to do in pursuit of our dreams.

The Dream in Question

Let's take the example of a car. Not just an ordinary production-line model, but the kind of vintage machine that only comes on the market every so often. Now, to successfully acquire that vehicle, you will need to do a number of things for yourself. You will need to find out where it can be purchased and perhaps persuade a reluctant owner to sell. You'll also require some cash. To ensure the money is there, you might have to sell another classic, work some overtime or – if you already run a business – have a particularly good month in terms of selling to your existing customers or attracting new ones. There are a lot of moving parts.

So how does the law of attraction help, given you're doing a lot of work? Sometimes, the assistance takes the form of serendipity. There aren't too many cars like this on the market, and you only find one available because of a chance encounter with an acquaintance of the seller at the supermarket checkout. Cars come up in the conversation because said acquaintance is carrying a motoring mag. More directly, you might find the money is available because of a windfall or inheritance. The law of attraction smooths your way.

To give another example, let's say money itself is the goal. The law of attraction could help you achieve it – again – through a windfall. But it could also be that other doors open, in the form of a promotion, job or business opportunity. Things begin to fall into place.

Celebrity Advocates

At this point, let's move away from hypotheticals and into some real-world – and very well-known – examples.

Witness Jim Carrey. One of the world's most renowned actors, he does comedy and drama to equally impressive effect. But like most actors, there was a time when he was neither rich nor successful. He was just another Hollywood hopeful, nursing a burning ambition.

So he set himself a goal – in this case, a financial one. By his own account, Carrey deployed a visualization technique as a means to drive his career forward. Put simply, he wrote himself a cheque for $10 million and post-dated it several years ahead. The aim in part was to send a message to himself and the universe that his ambition was not simply to make a living as an actor, but that he was bent on multimillion-dollar success. Years later, when he retrieved the post-dated cheque, he'd just found out his next film would make him $10 million.

In law of attraction terms, it was a clever move. Visualizing success, or even creating the image of something as solid as a car, can be tricky. Carrey sidestepped that by creating his own visual image that he could carry around. And it told a story about his future.

Now, Jim Carrey didn't write that cheque and just sit back to wait for the roles to come rushing in. He doubtless attended auditions and honed his acting. But in visualizing success – a key element of the law of attraction – he put down a marker that made his desired outcome more likely.

Lady Gaga deployed a different kind of visualization technique while also affirming her belief in herself. Essentially, she created a mantra that went something like this: 'Music is my life. The fame is inside of me. I'm going to make a number-one record with number-one hits.' It was a way of reprogramming herself to make success much more likely. However, like Jim Carrey, she then put the work in.

A Two-Way Process

In that respect, achieving success through the law of attraction is a two-way process. In visualizing or focusing on a goal, you are not only asking the universe for help but also reprogramming your own thought processes. As you become positively focused on your goal, the greater the likelihood is that you will achieve it.

There are really no limits on what you can achieve or acquire. But everyone is different. We – all of us – have different definitions of what success looks like, which in turn tends to shape what we want out of life. And as individuals, we change. What's important to us today may not matter very much at all in ten years' time.

Happily, the law of attraction is infinitely adaptable. If your goal is to find a happy relationship, it can help you achieve that. If you need money, the law of attraction is on hand to help. For those who are seeking to build businesses, the law of attraction is a tool that can be used to assist in finding customers, identifying and securing investment, or hooking up with a partner. It can even prove useful in helping you improve your mental and physical health.

How Does It Work?

But how does the law of attraction work? Is it a by-product of a self-help technique that essentially fosters a positive mental attitude – such as Lady Gaga's affirmation mantra – which ultimately makes success more likely? Or is there something deeper and more esoteric at work – some kind of universal force that can be tapped into and harnessed?

That's a difficult question to answer, but perhaps we don't need to. You don't have to be familiar with Albert Einstein's account of space-time or even Isaac Newton's law to observe the effects of gravity and know that it works.

Perhaps quantum physics offers a better analogy. When you get down to the level of subatomic particles, matter begins to behave very strangely. Particles act like waves, and waves behave like particles. Even more strange is a phenomenon known as quantum entanglement, where two particles can react to each other in real time regardless of where they are in space. Scientists don't know why these very small pieces of matter behave the way they do, but what they can do is observe the various phenomena and make cal-culations and predictions around such behaviour. The laws of quantum physics can then be harnessed to facilitate real-world tasks, such as building faster and more efficient computers.

I feel the same way about the law of attraction. I have seen it work in my own life. It has helped me achieve my ambitions, buy houses, grow businesses, marry my best friend – the list goes on. I don't necessarily know how it works exactly, but it does – provided that you follow certain rules. Later in this chapter, I'll set out a seven-step process to use the law of attraction to make improve-ments in your own life – through manifestation *and* action.

Making the Law of Attraction Work for You

At this point, you might be thinking, 'You know what – I'll give this a go. What have I got to lose?' On the other hand, you could be say-ing, 'This is a business book. What's with all this New Age stuff? I'm not buying this at all.'

Either way, I would simply suggest that you approach the next few pages with an open mind. Try some of the techniques I'm sug-gesting, and then decide whether the law of attraction will work for you.

First you'll need to identify something that you really want – let's say for the sake of simplicity that it's a material object. You ask for it and you visualize it (we'll be talking about that more in a minute) and run through the steps that will help you to bring that object into your life. And perhaps then you wait for a while – half expecting the law of attraction to set the necessary wheels in motion and half expecting to be disappointed. This is, after all, an experiment.

And that's where your attempt to harness the law of attraction probably begins and ends. A half-expectation of success is not enough. To make the law of attraction work for you, it's vital that you absolutely believe in the underlying principle. To put it another way, you can't fool the universe. If you are not convinced of the power of attraction – if you're only half convinced – then you are unlikely to see a result.

At this point, you might ask to be shown some evidence. Some proof that might prompt you to cast aside any doubt and put your trust in the power of attraction. That would be a fair request, but actually it's the wrong starting point.

These days, we're brought up and educated to think in terms of the scientific method. And a scientist will tell you that something is only a reality if it can be proven to be so. The same scientist might say: 'Show me that it's real and then I'll believe.' But the law of attraction requires a different approach, which can be summed up in the following sentence: 'Once you believe 100 per cent, then the universe will show you.'

This is really about the interface between frame of mind and the ability of an individual to use thought to influence material reality. Or you can think of it this way. Thoughts are themselves material things – they are certainly real – and they have their own frequency. By using that frequency, you can influence material reality. But only if you believe – really believe – that you can.

Belief is just one part – admittedly, a vital part – of a bigger equation. Harnessing the power of attraction is a conscious process. In my experience, there are seven important steps that you should follow.

Step One – Document Your Goals

First and foremost, you have to be clear about what you want to achieve. Most of us have a tendency to muddy the waters a little when we sit down to think about our goals. We start off thinking about a particular objective – let's say the successful conclusion of a business deal – and other thoughts rush in. Before too long, we find ourselves wrestling with multiple objectives. Some are important, some less so. In extreme cases, we can lose sight of what we really want or need and the path to obtaining it.

So, at the outset, it's important to focus on clearly defined goals.

In my experience, the best way to do this is to sit down with a pen and paper or laptop and document what you want to achieve. We covered this in depth in Chapter Two, so you should already have a considered and clear list of goals.

And once you've done that, read what you've written down out loud. And repeat those words again, and again. This technique – you can think of it as part of your mental toolkit – provides a means to reprogramme your mind. As you repeat your defined goals, you are affirming them; and that in turn creates a sense of certainty that you can and will achieve them. You are building belief.

Step Two – Ask

Documenting your goals builds a necessary foundation, but it doesn't necessarily start the building process. The next step along the law of attraction road is, quite simply, to ask for what you want. Now, you could couch this in terms of asking a higher power. Or you might describe it as asking the universe to give you what you want. Whatever your belief system, the important thing is simply to ask. This is the point where aspiration requires action.

Remember, stick to the documented goals, do them one at a time, and keep those goals specific and measurable.

Step Three – Visualize

For many people, this will be the toughest part of the attraction process. The thinking behind visualization is simple. By concentrating on a visual aspect of the desired outcome – signing a contract with a big customer; buying the house you've always wanted; getting the money you need to complete a project – you are making it real. In essence, when you visualize successfully you are creating a kind of pre-memory. The event has already happened. It's part of your life. You've seen the object with your eyes and you've held it in your hands.

But that presupposes an ability to visualize. Again, the brain isn't always helpful. You'll sit down and attempt to visualize an object, and other thoughts begin to rush in.

The answer – for many people – will be to deploy meditative techniques. Choose a time when you are unlikely to be interrupted. Sit down on a chair – avoiding one that will encourage you to lean back too far – and breathe deeply. Concentrate on your breath until you're relaxed. Once you are, begin to visualize what you want to obtain.

If it's a car, for instance, see everything about it in your mind's eye. Then go further. Imagine what the steering wheel feels like in your hands. But don't leave it at that. Visualization is a powerful tool, but remember there is a real and tactile world out there. If the goal is a material object – and not all goals are – in a material universe you have the advantage of being able to visit and interact with whatever it is that you wish to acquire.

As mentioned in the chapter on goal setting, if your goal is a new car, visit a showroom. Take the make and model you want out for a test drive. If your sights are set on a dream home, go out into the real world – perhaps starting on a property website – and find the properties that match your specifications and your visualization.

This is an important part of the process. On one level, you are proving to yourself that what you visualized actually exists and can be acquired. That might be obvious in the case of a mass-produced item such as a car, but less so if the goal is a home with very specific features within a certain geographical area, in which case finding the right sort of property and walking around it will help you take another step towards turning your vision into a tangible reality.

You are feeling what it is like to walk into the kind of home you've always wanted. You are experiencing the way your dream car takes a corner. Or, in the case of something smaller but equally desirable, you are feeling a Swiss watch on your wrist and seeing the workmanship up close.

Step Four – Adopt the Right Mindset

Let's pause for breath and return to the importance of belief. At this point, you've decided on your goal, you've asked for it, you've visualized it and you've taken the first positive steps to obtaining it.

But mindset is all-important. If we go back to that basic principle of the law of attraction – namely that you draw in what you give out – it's crucial to align your own mindset with what you hope to attain.

This is partly a matter of believing in the process itself, as we discussed earlier, but positivity and happiness are also key. It's hard – perhaps even impossible – to imagine a situation where the law of attraction could work positively for someone who approaches life in a negative frame of mind.

One of my clients was planning to run an event, but she was blocking herself. Her fear was that not enough people would turn up. There was a real danger of creating a self-fulfilling prophecy. Fear that the event might not be well supported could have led to its cancellation.

A change of mindset was needed. A belief that people would come. The event did take place, and it was a great success.

In my experience, success tends to come to those who are not only positive and happy but also consistently grateful for everything that life has given them to date. You attract what you are.

Step Five – Take Action

We touched on this earlier in the chapter, but it's worth stressing again and again that the law of attraction requires more than visualization. It will help you to achieve your goals, but you shouldn't regard it as a magic trick. Work is required.

If you want to start a business, you cannot just think about it – you have to get out there and start doing it. If you want to publish a book, you have to write the proposal and eventually the book. If you want to find a romantic partner, you cannot just sit in your home waiting for them to appear at your front door, you have to get out there and start meeting people or pay for matchmaking. Visualization and manifestation still require action.

The universe will help you get what you want, and there are occasions when the desired outcome will simply manifest. But for the most part, the law of attraction works in tandem with the work that you do for yourself.

So when you've decided on and visualized your goals, create an action plan. Ask yourself how you can create the circumstances that will allow you to fulfil your objectives. And then put your plan into action.

Step Six – Receive

This is the simplest of the steps. After all your good work, you achieve your objective. Be grateful.

Step Seven – Repeat

Now is the time to return to the goals you documented in step one. This is the point at which you choose what to focus on next, and repeat the process outlined above.

Getting Started/Tasks

If you believe in the law of attraction, it will work for you. To take the next step, go back to the goals that we discussed in Chapter Two. Choose one and start the seven steps.

The Bit about Karma

We're almost at the end of the book. Maybe you picked it up looking for inspiration when your business idea was nothing more than a concept. Or perhaps you were already some way down the entre-preneurial road, enjoying the journey and the fruits of success.

If that's the case, you will have already acquired a huge amount of knowledge and experience – some coming from this book, we hope, but much of it drawn from the challenges you've faced and overcome.

So, what next?

Well, one of the most valuable things you can do is pass that knowledge on to others. Not everyone gets this far. Many people could use help and advice. As your success grows, your experience can play a crucial role in helping others to succeed.

Realizing that you have something to offer is, in fact, one of the milestones on your own road to success. In the early days, you might well spend time seeking help from others – a family friend who runs a business, a mentor or a partner.

And then something changes. You find that you are being asked to give keynote speeches at industry events or to sit on panels. You might be asked to be a mentor yourself or (further down the line) join a young company's board as a non-executive director. You are sought out at networking events, and you receive emails asking for advice.

This is all good, but at first it can seem overwhelming. You have a business to run, so do you necessarily want to spend time – valuable time – passing knowledge on to others?

The first thing that has to be said is that providing help to others as a speaker or coach can become part of your career. Something that helps pay the bills. Equally, though, advising others on a pro bono basis is a good thing – as long as you don't allow it to knock you off course.

On one level, you can think of it as karma. In a spiritual sense, the idea behind karma is that our actions (and perhaps also our thoughts) not only affect others but reflect back on ourselves, either positively or negatively. Broadly speaking – very broadly – if you perform good and positive deeds, then you will be rewarded with good fortune. Negative deeds have the opposite effect.

You don't have to be a mystic to see how this works. Let's look at an example. A young man takes a job as a salesman. He's good at closing deals, but not necessarily ethical. For a while, it works and sales are good. But over time he notices that he's trusted less – not just by clients but by everyone. His lack of ethics has had a consequence.

So let's stay positive. Purely in terms of self-interest alone, taking the time and trouble to help others brings great rewards. And it's not only about reputation. If you help others, they will be more willing to help you. You are building a community.

Helping others also enhances your own personal development. Let's say you're asked to speak at an event on the subject of boot-strapping a business. This is something that you've done, but not really thought about. Somehow – back in the early days – you winged it. But today, you're imparting knowledge to others. So you have to think more carefully about what you did right and (crucially) the things that didn't go so well.

You are, in effect, not only providing insights for others, but also becoming more self-aware in the process. What's more, the people in the audience will ask some searching questions. Answering them requires more analysis. You are growing.

But when is it right to charge money for your advice, and when should you offer it for free? That's a tricky one. It's always good to take time to speak to people when they approach you. But you may wish to set a time limit for a free consultation on a topic pertaining to your expertise, for example a fifteen-minute call.

Some event organizers will ask you to appear for free (or perhaps for expenses) while you are building a reputation, and you may consider it to be worthwhile – assuming, of course, there is some form of value-add (a worthy audience, testimonials, access to data, etc.). On the other hand, if public speaking becomes part of your portfolio, then it's important to have charging policies.

However, it's probably worth remembering that some advice can be imparted fairly quickly. As a rule of thumb: information for free; implementation for a fee. In other words, if you are being asked to get under the hood of someone's business, you should probably be racking up some billable hours.

Becoming a Mentor or Coach

One way to make a real difference to individuals is to become either a mentor or a coach.

The two terms are often used interchangeably, but actually mentors and coaches do different things. Generally speaking, mentors develop long-term relationships with their mentees. Very often, the mentor has strong industry knowledge that they can impart; over time, this knowledge is shared, helping the mentee to grow and negotiate challenges. A coach usually has a more specific role. Let's say you're a business founder and you realize that closing sales isn't your strong point. A coach will focus on that particular weakness and help you overcome it.

To put it another way, a coach helps get something out of you, and a mentor shares information and provides you with an action plan for success. A key role of the mentor is to help you recognize and deal with blind spots and weaknesses. We have mentored a lot of businesses over the years, using our experience to prevent business owners from making mistakes and helping them elevate their business or business idea to solidify their success.

In truth, neither of us used mentors as much as we should have in our early days, but there were other sources of information. For instance, I used consultants, which are not quite the same thing but nonetheless served a similar purpose.

The important thing to remember is that there is an ecosystem of mentors, coaches, consultants and public speakers who are out there sharing their knowledge. As you become more successful, you will have opportunities to become part of that ecosystem. This is often described as 'paying it forward', or as a gift to the upcoming generation. But it's a gift to yourself as well.

ENTREPRENEUR INSIGHT:
Leaving a Legacy

*It's always worth remembering that you can make a real difference
in the world. When Yvette Noel-Schure began working as a publicist
in the record industry, she was – amazingly – the only black
publicist at Sony. 'Ten years after me leaving, there isn't a black
publicist,' she says now.*

*So one way that Yvette can leave a legacy – or make a difference –
is simply by being who she is: a black woman and a very
high-profile success story. She is the publicist who makes things
happen for Beyoncé, as well as for a host of other major musical
stars. Her success has created an industry slogan, intended to be a
rallying cry: 'Beyoncé's Publicist is Black.' I even saw this
emblazoned on a fan's jacket at a recent Beyoncé concert.*

*But equally important, Yvette is a teacher. Every year she teaches
a week of classes at the Berklee College of Music campus in
Valencia. 'It's just a week, but I put those students to work,' she
says with relish.*

*It's her way of paying forward her own success, and of inspiring
the next generation who will be the movers and shakers in her
industry in years to come.*

It's F**king Emotional

Much of what we've covered in this book probably seems a long
way from the world of business plans, raising finance, dealing with
cash flow and paying taxes – the technical issues that confront
founders as they build their dreams.

That is deliberate. Our first book, *Self Made: The Definitive Guide
to Business Startup Success*, was written as a practical, no-nonsense

guide to starting and running your own company. This time around, we wanted to do something very different but no less practical.

Because here's the truth of the matter: running a business is a f**king emotional rollercoaster ride. You encounter success, failure, setbacks and personal difficulties, while at the same time learning a lot about your own strengths and weaknesses. These are the tangible realities of business. Yes, to run a company you need to understand how to write a business plan, how to sell and how to manage cash. But you also need the mental strength and resilience to cope with anything, from a pandemic taking away a big percentage of your income, to social media campaigns, to trolls who not only attack the business but also you personally. You need emotional intelligence too, to manage relationships with customers, stakeholders and romantic partners.

And, ultimately, you should enjoy the ride. Remember that feeling we talked about in an earlier chapter – the one when you get off a big rollercoaster? You're a little shell-shocked, maybe even unsteady on your feet. Your friend says, 'Let's get a drink and relax.'

'No,' you reply, 'I want to go again.'

That's the game.